MONITORING SUSTAINABILITY

About the Author

Dr. Nira Ramachandran is an alumnus of the Jawaharlal Nehru University, New Delhi. She has been trained in her field of specialization both in India and abroad. She has been associated as researcher and teacher with several institutions including the Indian Institute of Management, Bangalore as a Research Fellow, as Assistant Professor in Bangalore University, as CSIR Fellow in Delhi University, and as the Coordinator of the Centre for Sustainable Development at the Lal Bahadur Shastri National Academy of Aministration, Mussoorie.

In 1996 she was awarded an ICSSR Senior Fellowship, the research output of which culminated in this book. She is the author of several papers on developmental issues including carrying capacity, food security and wild life conservation.

MONITORING SUSTAINABILITY
Indices and Techniques of Analysis

NIRA RAMACHANDRAN

CONCEPT PUBLISHING COMPANY PVT. LTD.
NEW DELHI-110059

ISBN: 978-81-7022-816-5

First Published 2000
Reprinted 2001, 2002

Published and Printed by

Concept
Since 1974

Concept Publishing Company Pvt. Ltd.
A/15-16, Commercial Block, Mohan Garden,
New Delhi-110059 (India)
T: 91-11-41101460
E: publishing@conceptpub.com, *W*: www.conceptpub.com

IN MEMORY

OF

MY PARENTS

PREFACE

The book is the outcome of a research project sponsored by the Indian Council of Social Science Research under its Senior Fellowship Scheme.

While the need for re-assessing development in terms of environmental sustainability needs no re-iteration, methods and techniques of carrying out such an analysis are often too complex, requiring sophisticated tools and specialised knowledge. This book is an attempt at providing simple techniques for appraising the sustainability of development at various levels of an economy using easily available data from published sources. It also suggests methods of generating data at the micro-level, where secondary data is not available, using both statistical and participatory techniques. It is hoped that this would prove a useful guide for researchers, planners and administrators dealing with development planning at all levels.

The study would not have been possible without the sponsorship of the Indian Council of Social Science Research, the Institutional Affiliation and support of initially, the Lal Bahadur Shastri National Academy of Administration (LBSNAA), Mussoorie and later the National Society for Promotion of Development Administration, Research and Training (NSDART), Mussoorie.

I would also like to record my appreciation of the assistance rendered by Mr. R. K. Bhardwaj for data collection. Ms. Meenakshi Arora, Ms. Sangeeta Thapa and Ms. Ingita Aswal for secretarial assistance. Ms. Seema Joshi provided the cartographic inputs. Finally, the project owes its completion to the constant advice and encouragement of my husband, Professor H. Ramachandran.

February 1999
Mussoorie

NIRA RAMACHANDRAN

CONTENTS

LIST OF TABLES

LIST OF MAPS AND GRAPHS

1

SUSTAINABILITY
Developing the Concept

Evolution of the Concept

Left to herself, Nature ensures a dynamic balance in the global eco-system. Demand and supply regulate each other and the balance, while teetering heavily in favour of one or the other for a time, eventually regains equilibrium. Take for example, a forest eco-system with a population of deer. As the number of deer increase, grazing conditions deteriorate, deer migrate to other areas, the pressure reduces, pasture begins to rejuvenate and the eco-system is in perfect balance again. Natural equilibrium forms the basis of the Malthusian hypothesis which, in essence, equates mankind and his habitat with a natural eco-system.

The natural resource base, on which the various successively higher levels of the eco-system depend, has its limits, which are expressed in terms of carrying capacities. One hectare of pasture land can support a certain number of cattle, one square kilometre of forest is required to support a tiger, a fraction of an hectare of cropland under traditional intensive cultivation can just support a tropical farmer and his family of five at a subsistence level. While a single eco-system with its dependent animal population lends itself to calculations of carrying capacities with comparative ease, the intricate interlinkages and complexities of human population do not permit the same ease of approach. Primitive man, out to satisfy his needs for food and shelter, was closer to Nature and thus lent himself to analysis by more or less the same rules as the rest of the animal kingdom. Modern man, however, armed with powerful technology and his vast numbers presents a complex problem with no simple solutions.

The first notion of sustainability arose when the rapid growth of human population began to outpace the production of food. The idea of a world overflowing with people, where both food and space would fall short of their requirements, began to emerge. The club of Rome's (Meadows *et al.*, 1972) hypothesis stemmed from this viewpoint. However, decades after the dire predictions of doomsday had passed, mankind was still thriving on the face of the earth. The role of technology in staving off the inevitable began to emerge and the techno-centred approach to sustainability took shape

If sustainability were a mere trade off between ever-growing populations and a static or even diminishing resource base, monitoring sustainability would be simple, maintaining it merely a question of keeping the population within the limits set by technology and nature. But estimating demand is now no longer a function of simple growth. It is compounded by the disproportionate growth in demands as a result of globalisation, communications and the exposure of the hitherto insular populace to international tastes and living standards. As a result, in the developing world, the vast majority are yet to achieve minimum levels of nutrition, shelter, health and livelihoods, while a newly created burgeoning urban middle class with sudden access to inflated incomes and a consumerist lifestyle are gathered in out sized metropolises consuming a disproportionate share of the country's resources. Taking the case of India itself, about 27 per cent of the country's vast population lives in urban areas. Of this, about 30 per cent fall into the middle and upper income groups i.e., a total of 125 million people whose excessive demands for water, power and fuel lie at the roots of the unsustainability in the country. The country as a whole, in its quest for development and improved quality of life also makes increasing demands on the resource base which are over and above the legitimate demands imposed by a growing population. Thus, emerging within the developing countries, is a divide no less defined than the North-South divide between the 'haves' and the 'havenots' the polluters and the sufferers—i.e. the divide between the affluent sections (largely urban) and the vast majority comprising of the rural poor.

The spate of pollution related disasters from the 70s, acid rain, grossly polluted river waters, nuclear spill over and the free entry of harmful ultra-violet rays into the atmosphere as a result of the hole in the protective ozone layer caused a panic reaction in the developed world. For the first time, awoke the realisation that the future of the entire global community was at stake. Environmental linkages are such that unchecked activity in any one part of the world can affect the entire globe. No country can live in isolation any longer.

International Concerns

The Stockholm Conference held in 1972 crystallised this thinking in 'Only One Earth' the book written in preparation for the Conference. The concept of 'Spaceship Earth' used by Boulding (1966) became commonplace. The fundamental point emerging from the Stockholm Conference was that, development need not be impaired by environmental protection, but could be achieved through integrated development planning and planning efforts to resolve conflicts between environment and development. The Conference, however, stressed on the need to resolve conflicts. without actually demonstrating how.

The most conspicuous result of the Conference, however, was the creation of the United Nations Environment Programme (UNEP) in December 1972 to deal with environmental issues. The UNEP has several notable achievements to its credit, but the one most significant for the idea of sustainable development is the meeting of experts held at Cocoyoc in Mexico in October 1974. This achieved what the Stockholm Conference with its classic First World environmental concerns of industrialisation and pollution, did not. It looked at environmental problems from the perspective of the Third World, particularly the Third World poor. The resulting Cocoyoc Declaration emphasized the problem of mal distribution of resources and underlined the inner limits of human needs as well as the outer limits of resource depletion. It pointed to basic needs and called for a redefinition of development goals and global lifestyles. The UNEP and the World Wildlife Fund also financed the World Conservation Strategy (WCS), which was prepared by the IUCN. The WCS was the culmination of more than two decades of thinking by conservationists, about ways to further nature conservation on a global scale. It was aimed at government policy makers, conservationists and development practitioners and offered both an intellectual framework and practical guidance' (IUCN, 1980).

The World Conservation Strategy (WCS) identified three objectives for conservation. First is the maintenance of essential ecological processes. These are 'governed,' supported or strongly moderated by ecosystems and are essential for food production, health and other aspects of human survival and sustainable development. They are called 'life-support systems' and include agricultural land and soil, forests, and coastal and freshwater ecosystems. The second objective is the preservation of genetic diversity in different varieties of locally adapted crop plants or livestock including wild species. This genetic diversity is both an insurance (for example against crop diseases) and an investment for the future (e.g. crop breeding or pharmaceuticals). The WCS's third objective is the sustainable development of species and ecosystems, particularly fisheries, wild species which are cropped, forests and timber resources and grazing land (Table 1.1).

The objectives were then broken down into a list of priority requirements, drawn up on the basis of three criteria.

— significance – how important is it?
— urgency – how fast is it getting worse; and
— irreversibility

The WCS also discusses priorities for national action based on the preparation of separate national strategies (by governments or NGOs) which review development objectives in the light of the conservation objectives and establish priority requirements, identify obstacles and propose cost-effective ways of overcoming them, determining priority ecosystems and species for conservation and establishing a practical plan of action (Adams, 1990).

The establishment in December 1983 of the World Commission on Environment and Development at the call of the UN General Assembly brought the sustainable development debate into the economic and political context of international development. The Commission in its report 'Our Common Future' commonly known as the Bruntland Report (WCED, 1987) starts from the premise that development and environment cannot be separated. 'The environment does not exist as a sphere separate from human actions, ambitions and needs'. It is, therefore, futile

TABLE 1.1: **Priority Requirements of the World Conservation Strategy**

A. Ecological Processes

1. Reserve good cropland for crops (para 5.1)
2. Manage cropland to high, ecologically sound standards (para 5.3)
3. Ensure that the principal management goal for watershed forests and pastures is protection of the watershed
4. Ensure that the principal management goal for coastal wetlands is the maintenance of the processes on which the fisheries depend (para 5.6)
5. Control the discharge of pollutants (para 5.8)

B. Genetic Diversity

1. Prevent the extinction of species (para 6.1)
2. Preserve as many kinds as possible of crop plants, forage plants, timber trees, livestock, animals for aquaculture, microbes and other domestic organisms and their wild relatives (para 6.4)
3. Ensure on-site preservation programmes protect
   — the wild relatives of economically valuable and other useful plants and animals and their habitats
   — the habitats of threatened and unique species
   — unique ecosystems
   — representative samples of ecosystem types (para 6.8)
4. Determine the size, distribution and management of protected areas on the basis of the needs of the ecosystem and the plant and animal communities they are intended to protect (para 6.10)
5. Coordinate national and international protected area programmes (para 6.12)

C. Sustainable Utilisation

1. Determine the productive capacities of exploited species and ecosystems and ensure that utilisation does not exceed those capacities (para 7.1)
2. Adopt conservation management objectives for the utilisation of species and ecosystems (para 7.2)
3. Ensure that access to a resource does not exceed the resource's capacity to sustain exploitation (para 7.3)
4. Reduce excessive yields to sustainable levels (para 7.4)
5. Reduce incidental take as much as possible (para 7.5)
6. Equip subsistence communities to utilise resources sustainably (para 7.6)
7. Maintain the habitats of resource species (para 7.7)
8. Regulate international trade in wild animals and plants (para 7.8)
9. Allocate timber concessions with care and manage them to high standards (para 7.9)
10. Limit firewood consumption to sustainable levels (para 7.10)
11. Regulate the stocking of grazing lands to maintain the long term productivity of plants and animals (para 7.11)
12. Utilise indigenous wild herbivores, alone or with livestock, where domestic stock alone would degrade the environment.

Source: IUCN/1980.

to attempt to deal with environmental problems without a broader perspective that encompasses the factors underlying world poverty and international inequality'.

Thus the definition of sustainable development, here, rests on two basic premises – one that development action must have as its focus the poor, thus giving rise to the concept of basic needs, and second, the idea that environmental limits are not set by the environment itself, but by technology and social organisation. Environment and Development policies must be restructured to allow nations to move from their present, often destructive, processes of growth and development onto sustainable development paths. Critical objectives for policy making that flow from the concept of sustainable development include:

1. Reviving growth
2. Changing the quality of growth
3. Meeting essential needs for jobs, food, energy, water and sanitation
4. Ensuring a sustainable level of population
5. Conserving and enhancing the resource base
6. Reorienting technology and managing risk
7. Merging environment and economics in decision-making.

Referring to the Bruntland Report, Bartelmus says "What is new is the approach, advocated for implementing sustainable development. This approach calls for a move from dealing with environmental effects after their occurrence to focussing on the policy sources of these effects for preventive action. This can also be seen as a shift from a discussion of environment and development to development and environment. In other words, this is an attempt to merge environmental issues with mainstream policy making rather than to change those policies from the periphery of the environmental movement" (Bartelmus, 1994). He goes on to say that "What is needed now is to replace dramatisation and rhetorics with scientific measurements, synthesised into statistics and indicators that provide a comprehensive picture of sustainability or non-sustainability of current human activities."

Measuring Sustainability: Approaches

Attempts at measuring sustainability began in the 1980s. Turning the concept into practical measurable reality was the natural outcome of the acceptance of the concept. As the concept of sustainable development gained widespread acceptance, the need to identify indicators and methods for assessing the level of sustainability of a country or a region began to gain currency. Measuring sustainability in quantitative terms resolves itself into two approaches – (a) The inclusion of natural resource capital into national accounts; and (b) The development of indicators or sets of indicators to assess the sustainability of the development path.

Natural Resource Accounting

While conventional economics has treated the environment as external to its analysis, the realisation of the inter-dependence of economy and environment gave rise to a rethinking of conventional economic thought. This led to the concept of green accounting as a solution to integrating environmental and economic data and analytical variables (Bartelmus, 1994).

The original ecological concept of sustainability was defined as 'prudent behaviour by a predator that avoids over exploiting its prey to ensure an optimum sustained yield' (Odum, 1971). Translated into economics, it became the concept of income as a similar guide for prudent conduct in spending recurrent monetary receipts. Generalising this notion for the whole population of a country yields a concept of national income as the amount a population can consume during a period of time without impoverishing itself. Thus the existing system of national accounting which deals with stocks and flows of economic transactions but excludes the depletion of natural resources and the degradation of environmental quality from its analysis cannot be used to measure the sustainability of the growth process. In fact, 'an expanding economy based on such an accounting system would be expected to slowly undermine itself, eventually collapsing as support systems are destroyed' (Brown, 1993).

The major drawbacks in conventional accounts pointed out by Repetto and others are given below:

1. The neglect of scarcities of natural resources which threaten the sustained productivity of the economy;
2. The neglect of the degradation of environmental quality from pollution and other human activity and its effects on human health and welfare; and
3. Accounting for environmental protection expenditures (defensive expenditures) as increases in national income and product, even though those expenditures could be considered as social costs rather than social progress (Repetto, *et al.*, 1989).

Notable efforts at green accounting include the United Nations System of National Accounts, the SNA (Inter-Secretarial Working Group, 1994) which includes in its asset accounts non-produced natural resources that provide economic benefits to their owners. While there is yet no international consensus on how to incorporate, comprehensively, environmental costs and benefits in national accounts, the central framework of the SNA could well become a starting point for environmental accounting (Bartelmus, 1994).

While replacement of the well-established conventional system of national accounts may be premature, the use of environmental and natural resources accounting as a complement to the existing system, in the form of satellite accounts is certainly possible. In fact, UNCED in its Agenda 21, requested that all member-states of the United Nations establish integrated environmental and economic accounting as a complement to traditional national accounting practices for the foreseeable future. (United Nations, 1993a). Satellite systems of national accounts serve to expand the analytic capacity of national accounting for selected areas of social concern without overburdening or disrupting the core-system (Schafer and Stahmer, 1990).

The Statistical Division of the United Nations (UNSTAT) has developed methodologies for a (satellite) system of integrated Environmental and Economic Accounting (SEEA) in an SNA handbook (United Nations, 1993b) with the following objectives:

— identification of all environment related flows and stocks in conventional national accounts;
— incorporation of environmental costs and benefits into

national accounts;

— accounting for the maintenance of national wealth;

— compilation of environmentally—adjusted macro economic indicators, notably an environmentally adjusted net-domestic product (EDP).

National resource accounts were pioneered in Norway (Alfsen, Bye and Lorentsen, 1987). They present physical stocks of natural resources at the beginning of an accounting period and the stocks at the end of the period. Natural patrimony accounting developed in France (Theys, 1989), is broader, both in the sense of covering natural assets and in including, in principle, other monetary accounting approaches (Bartelmus, 1994).

Indicators of Sustainability

National resource accounting led to the development of one indicator - the EDP or environmentally adjusted net domestic product. This attempts at replacing the universally used NDP (net domestic product), as an indicator of development, with an indicator which reflects the sustainability of the development path, as well as the level of development itself. While laudable as an attempt towards assessing sustainability, it has yet to gain general acceptance. Several attempts at developing indicators or sets of indicators comprising of two or three variables, which reflect different dimensions of sustainability, have been made. As sustainable development is a multi-dimensional concept, such indicators would have to reflect all the dimensions involved. The basic dimensions of sustainable development would include:

— compilation of economic aggregates in per capita terms;

— definition of an overall human development index; and

— an assessment of the carrying capacity of land for human populations (Bartelmus, 1994).

Sustainability in terms of economic growth would require a growth rate which is at least equal to the population growth rate. While per capita G.N.P. is usually taken as an indicator of economic growth, it has little meaning unless its distribution among the population is also considered. This gives rise to the concept of equity or equitable distribution of the fruits of economic growth. Not only is equitable distribution necessary for development in the true sense, but economic inequities are frequently associated with non-economic (environmental) ones. Inequalities within and among countries are aggravated by denying the poor and under privileged access to increasingly scarce natural resources and by uneven spatial and social distribution of the impacts and costs of environmental degradation, (Bartelmus, 1994). For instance, gender bias in the distribution of work, income and wealth, especially in rural subsistence communities, has been blamed for depriving women of the results of economic growth and making them suffer the brunt of pressure on forests and crop lands (Jacobson, 1993).

'The incorporation of environmental concerns in development planning and policy formulation requires the introduction of space as an explicit dimension of an integrative framework' (Bartelmus, 1994). The dimension of space must be introduced at least at three levels. At the local level, sustainability of development and of development planning must be rooted in the carrying capacity of the region. However, carrying capacity is also a function of the needs and aspirations of the population being carried. Thus the necessity for a participatory approach to assessing carrying capacities and planning for sustainable development. The central role of the government in socio-economic policy-making and planning and in the integration of environmental concerns, underlines the importance of regional/administrative boundaries in sustainable development planning.

The Human Development Index (HDI) of the United Nations Development Programme (UNDP), introduced in 1990 claims to be a measure of human progress by combining National Income with two other indicators that of adult literacy and life expectancy. Further adjustment for gender sensitivity and income distribution are also made and the inclusion of a Human Freedom Index reflecting various human rights is suggested. Assuming that the Index covers the most relevant development concerns and attaches correct weights to them, non-declining HDI would indeed reflect a sustained human development path (Bartelmus, 1994).

However, the sustainability issues cannot be divorced from the land and environment or eco-system within which a population lives and derives its livelihood. In this sense, the concept of carrying capacity emerges as basic to the measurement of sustainability. The number of people that can be sustained by a given region can be termed its carrying capacity. This capacity also depends on the desirable quality of life of the people which would have to be further defined in terms of basic needs or desirable standards. Identifying carrying capacities would also draw attention to non-sustainable trends in population growth or, even more so, in the demands being made by the population. As Hardin points out "Cultural carrying capacity and the standard of living are inversely related. The higher the standard of living, the fewer the number of people who can enjoy it" (Hardin, 1991).

However, apart from a few carrying capacity studies focussed on food and fuelwood (FAO, UNFPA and IIASA, 1982, World Bank 1985) carrying capacity analyses have not been widely applied in development research and analysis.

The Daly-Cobb Index of sustainable economic welfare (Daly and Cobb, 1990) attempts to incorporate the dimension of environment into the index. The index is built on three factors—average consumption, distribution and environmental degradation. The consumption component of the index is adjusted for distributional inequality after which environmental costs associated with factors such as the depletion of non-renewable resources, loss of farmland through erosion and urbanisation, loss of wetlands and the cost of air and water pollution are included. An attempt is also made to incorporate 'long-term environmental damage' such as the effects of global warming and of damage to the ozone layer.

Applied to the United States, the ISEW shows a rise in welfare per person of about 42 per cent between 1950 and 1976 after which a decline sets in registering a fall of about 12 per cent by 1988. The principal weakness of this method lies in the fact that it is dependent on data that is available only for a few countries.

The Sustainable Livelihood Security Index (Saleth, 1994) is based on causal relationship between livelihood, quality of life and sustainable development within the framework of carrying capacity. It develops a unified index based on a set of variables representing the three dimensions of economy, ecology and equity and ranks the various regions against the overall index as well as against specific aspects such as equity, in an attempt to identify the potential of each region for sustainable livelihood security, as well as to define the lines on which development should be planned.

Turning the concept of sustainability into policy raises fundamental questions about how to assess the well-being of present and future generations. The issue becomes more complex as future generations will inherit negative legacies like pollution, and resource depletion, as well as the wealth of knowledge, technology, skills and capital which we bequeath to them. This calls for measures sensitive enough to capture the fragile balance between development and sustainable development.

Stemming from the foregoing discussion the following points emerge:

— The future of mankind lies in sustainable development.
— Sustainability must be maintained at all levels - local regional, national and global
— To incorporate the concept of sustainability into planning, present levels of development must be remeasured in terms of sustainability.
— Measurement implies the selection of suitable indicators, which can capture the sensitivity of the environment to the development process.
— An index is only as good as its replicability. Thus an attempt must be made to select indicators based on data which is readily available at all levels and in all places.
— As environmental data is not readily available, proxy indicators must be selected which reflect to the largest extent, the original indicator.

Keeping in view the above mentioned points, the broad objective of the present study is to develop sets of indicators which can be used to assess the sustainability of regions at various levels of the organisational hierarchy. Attempts are made to apply these indicators at the country level over space and over time, at the State or regional level, at sub-State or district level and finally at micro level taking up a rural and an urban case. Techniques of using these indicators can also vary from case to case incorporating both quantitative and graphical methods. Efforts have been made to keep the methods as simple as possible and restrict the data input to what is easily accessible. Step by step procedures are detailed and complete data sets are provided in the Appendices with a view to facilitate similar application in other regions. Broad guidelines for policy decisions have also been indicated.

Structure of the Book

The book is divided into six chapters. Chapter 1 is based on the intensive literature survey undertaken in the first phase of the project wherein the development of the concept and indicators for measurement are reviewed. Chapter 2 derives from the statistical analysis of selected indicators of sustainability at the national level. The time period covered is 45 years i.e. annually from 1951 - 1996. Chapter 3 compares the indices of sustainable development in different States of the country and attempts to draw inferences from the different development paths followed by different States with a view to aid policy formulation. Chapter 4 focuses on a single natural region the Central Himalayas comprising the States of Jammu and Kashmir, Himachal Pradesh and the hill districts of Uttar Pradesh. Data on 13 indicators including 7 development indicators and 6 environmental indicators is analysed which enables, inter-district comparisons of status of sustainability. Chapter 5 assesses sustainability at the micro level with two case studies employing different databases and different techniques of analysis. The rural area study uses participatory methods to develop indicators for assessing the sustainability of development projects in the Chakrata block of Dehradun district. The urban case study deals with population projections and demand estimates with carrying capacity calculations for the mountain resort town of Mussoorie. Chapter 6 sums up the findings of the study. A comprehensive Bibliography is appended.

2

ON DEVELOPING INDICES OF SUSTAINABILITY

Introduction

This chapter attempts to assess the status of quality of life of the population in relation to status of environment in India in comparison to other Asian countries particularly the SAARC group. Subsequently, an attempt is made to analyse the trends in India over the last four and a half decades with reference to questions such as: Where did the country stand with reference to both these dimensions at the beginning of the plan period? Did the development path, being followed, focus on improving the quality of life or on preventing environmental degradation?

The search for sustainable development often ends in rhetoric. While the concept of sustainability has now emerged from its nebulous form, the modalities of assessing sustainability still remain unclear. In other words, what exactly is implied by development, its connotations in terms of sustainability and the probability of capturing these dimensions remains uncertain.

Taking as a starting point the fact that sustainable development involves two dimensions–sustainability of the impacts of human development on natural resources (environment) and–development, the initial step towards assessing sustainability is the identification of indicators reflecting both these dimensions. Once suitable indicators have been developed, it becomes relatively easier statistically to construct one or more composite indices. However, the main problem in assessing sustainability lies in the fact that there are no specific norms or values against which the level of sustainable development of an economy can be measured.

A set of acceptable norms on a whole range of possible variables must evolve with research efforts of individual and institutional empirical research, for acceptability would depend on the ability of the indices to capture empirical reality.

Choice of Variables

The selection of variables forms the crux of the methodology. However, this would be limited by the ready availability of data, since there is not much point in selecting variables for which information is rarely accessible or expensive to generate. The second consideration is the spatial unit of analysis since different variables assume significance at various levels of inquiry. The third consideration is consistency of availability over a time period, since both the concepts are dynamic and cannot be captured with a single point data, except when the objective is a cross-sectional analysis. Keeping these two considerations in view, two sets of variables were finally arrived at – one reflecting the quality of life, the other, the quality of the environment (See Tables 2.1 and 2.2).

Quality of Life Indicators

Quality of life is a function of economic well-being as well as of access to basic amenities. It is now well recognised that GNP has limited capacity to capture various human dimensions of development and quality of life including equity aspects. Most developing countries have sharply skewed incomes as well as unequal access to basic amenities. In the light of these considerations, for purposes of cross-country comparisons, the following indicators have been selected. However, as can be seen, often data is not available for all countries for the same time period. The eleven variables are as follows:

1. Per capita GNP (1995)
2. Percentage urban to total population (1994)
3. Percentage of labour force in industry to total labour force (1990)
4. Per capita electricity consumption (KWH) (1994)
5. Adult literacy rate (1994)

TABLE 2.1: **Asia: Quality of Life Indicators**

	Country	GNP per capita 1995		Country	% Urban Pop. (1994)		Country	Per Capita Electricity Consumption (kWh) 1994		Country	Adult Literacy Rate 1994
	1			2			3			4	
1	Kuwait	17390	1	Kuwait	97	1	Kuwait	14178	1	Thailand	93.5
2	S. Arabia	7040	2	S. Arabia	80	2	S. Arabia	3826	2	Sri Lanka	90.1
3	Malaysia	3890	3	Malaysia	53	3	Thailand	2032	3	Indonesia	83.2
4	Thailand	2740	4.5	Pakistan	34	4	China	780	4	Malaysia	83
5	Indonesia	980	4.5	Indonesia	34	5	India	420	5	China	80.9
6	Sri Lanka	700	6	China	29	6	Pakistan	418	6	Kuwait	77.8
7	China	620	7	India	27	7	Indonesia	315	7	S. Arabia	61.8
8	Pakistan	460	8	Sri Lanka	22	8	Sri Lanka	242	8	India	51.2
9	Bhutan	420	9	Thailand	20	9	Bhutan	143	9	Bhutan	41.1
10	India	340	10	Bangladesh	18	10	Bangladesh	85	10	Bangladesh	37.3
11	Bangladesh	240	11	Nepal	13	11	Nepal	44	11	Pakistan	37.1
12	Nepal	200	12	Bhutan	6		Malaysia		12	Nepal	27

(*Contd.*)

TABLE 2.1: *(Contd.)*

	Country	Life Expectancy at Birth Years (1994)		Country	Infant Mortality Rate per '000 live births (1994)		Country	% Pop. with Access to Safe Water (1990-96)		Country	% Pop. with Access to Sanitation (1990-96)
	5			6			7			8	
1	Kuwait	75.2	1	Malaysia	12	1	Kuwait	100	1	Thailand	96
2	Sri Lanka	72.2	2	Sri Lanka	16	2	Bangladesh	97	2	Malaysia	94
3	Malaysia	71.2	3	Kuwait	17	3	S. Arabia	95	3	S. Arabia	86
4	S. Arabia	70.3	4	S. Arabia	27	4	Thailand	89	4	Bhutan	70
5	Thailand	69.5	5	Thailand	29	5	China		5	China	67
6	China	68.9	6	China	43	6	India	81	6	Sri Lanka	63
7	Indonesia	63.5	7	Indonesia	53	7	Malaysia	78	7	Indonesia	51
8	Pakistan	62.3	8	India	74	8	Pakistan	74	8	Bangladesh	48
9	India	61.3	9	Pakistan	80	9	Nepal	63	9	Pakistan	47
10	Bangladesh	56.4	10	Bangladesh	85	10	Indonesia	62	10	India	29
11	Nepal	55.3	11	Nepal	92	11	Bhutan	58	11	Nepal	18
12	Bhutan	51.5	12	Bhutan	113	12	Sri Lanka	57		Kuwait	

(Contd.)

TABLE 2.1: *(Contd.)*

	Country	Daily Calorie Supply per capita (1992)		Country	Food Consumption as % of Total HH Consumption (1994)		Country	% of Labour Force Industry (1990)
	9			10			11	
1	Malaysia	2884	1	Malaysia	23	1	Kuwait	25
2	Indonesia	2755	2	Thailand	30	2	Malaysia	23
3	S. Arabia	2751	3	Pakistan	37	3	Sri Lanka	21
4	China	2729	4	Sri Lanka	43	4	S. Arabia	20
5	Thailand	2443	5	Indonesia	48	5	Pakistan	19
6	India	2395	6	India	52	6.5	Bangladesh	16
7	Pakistan	2316	7	Nepal	57	6.5	India	16
8	Sri Lanka	2275	8	Bangladesh	59	8	China	15
9	Bangladesh	2019	9	China	61	9	Indonesia	14
10	Nepal	1957		Bhutan		10	Thailand	14
	Bhutan			S. Arabia		11	Bhutan	1
	Kuwait			Kuwait		12	Nepal	0

TABLE 2.2: **Asia: Quality of Environment Indicators**

	Country	% Traditional Fuel Consumption to total fuel Consumption (1993)		Country	% HH Energy from fuelwood (1990)		Country	% Forest Area to Total Area (1993)		Country	% Arable Land to Total Area (1993)
	1			2			3			4	
1	China	6	1	Pakistan	72	1	Malaysia	67.6	1	Bangladesh	65.6
2	Thailand	8	2	China	80	2	Bhutan	66	2	India	50.5
3	Pakistan	21	3	Bangladesh	83	3	Indonesia	58.7	3	Thailand	34.3
4	India	23	4.5	Nepal	84	4	Nepal	40.8	4	Pakistan	26.1
5	Indonesia	36	4.5	India	84	5	Sri Lanka	32	5	Nepal	16.5
6	Bangladesh	47	6	Sri Lanka	85	6	Thailand	26.3	6	Sri Lanka	14.2
7	Sri Lanka	53	7	Indonesia	86	7	India	20.8	7	Indonesia	9.9
8	Bhutan	85		Malaysia		8	China	13.5	8	China	9.6
9	Nepal	92		Bhutan		9	Bangladesh	13.2	9	Malaysia	3.2
	Malaysia			Thailand		10	Pakistan	4.4	10	Bhutan	2.4
	S. Arabia			S. Arabia		11	S. Arabia	0.8	11	S. Arabia	1.7
	Kuwait			Kuwait		12	Kuwait	0.1	12	Kuwait	0.3

(Contd.)

TABLE 2.2: *(Contd.)*

	Country	% Irrigated Land to Arable Land 1993		Country	% Annual Rate of deforestation (1981-90)		Country	% Annual Rate of reforestation (1981-90)		Country	Internal Renewable Water Resources per capita ('000 cu m per year) 1995
	5			6			7			8	
1	Pakistan	82.3	1.5	Pakistan	-2.9	1	Malaysia	35	1	Bhutan	58
2	Sri Lanka	59.1	1.5	Thailand	-2.9	2.5	Nepal	32	2	Malaysia	22.6
3	China	53.6	3	S. Arabia	-1.9	2.5	India	32	3	Indonesia	12.8
4	Kuwait	40	4	Malaysia	-1.8	4	Thailand	13	4	Nepal	7.8
5	Nepal	36.6	5	Sri Lanka	-1.3	5	Indonesia	12	5	Pakistan	3.3
6	Bangladesh	32.8	6.5	Nepal	-1	6	Bhutan	11	6	Thailand	3
7	Malaysia	32.7	6.5	Indonesia	-1	7	Sri Lanka	8	7	Bangladesh	2.5
8	Bhutan	29.6	8.5	Bhutan	-0.6	8	China	6	8	Sri Lanka	2.4
9	India	28.9	8.5	India	-0.6	9.5	Bangladesh	3	9	China	2.3
10	Thailand	25	10	China	-0.4	9.5	Pakistan	3	10	India	2.2
11	Indonesia	24.3	11	Bangladesh	10.7		S. Arabia			S. Arabia	
12	S. Arabia	11.9		Kuwait			Kuwait			Kuwait	

(Contd.)

TABLE 2.2: *(Contd.)*

	Country	Annual Marine Catch (% change since 1981-83 to 1991-93)		Country	CO_2 emissions (M. tonne/ per capita) 1992
		9			10
1	China	168	1	Nepal	0.1
2	Indonesia	71	2	Bangladesh	0.2
3	India	68	3	Sri Lanka	0.3
4	Pakistan	62	4	Pakistan	0.6
5	Thailand	52	5	India	0.9
6	Saudi Arabia	36	6	Indonesia	1
7	Bangladesh	15	7	Thailand	1.7
8	Sri Lanka	4	8	China	2.3
9	Malaysia	-13	9	Malaysia	3.8
	Bhutan		10	Kuwait	11.2
	Nepal		11	S. Arabia	13.1
	Kuwait		0	Kuwait	

6. Life expectancy at birth (years) (1994)
7. Infant mortality rate per '000 live births (1994)
8. Percentage of population with access to safe water (1990-96)
9. Percentage of population with access to sanitation (1990-96)
10. Daily calorie supply per capita (1992)
11. Food consumption as a percentage of total household consumption (1994)

Per Capita GNP

As a measure of economic health, perhaps, no better indicator exists than per capita GNP despite limitations in varying methods of accounting. The most widely used measure of economic progress, GNP plays an important role in national and international policies. However, it must be realised that GNP, NNP, etc., which form the basis of national income accounts, do not reflect the depletion and degradation of natural resources even when these resources are a primary source of income. This is particularly the case in the primary sector based economies of the developing countries.

Percentage Urban to Total Population and Percentage of Labour Force in Industry to Total Labour Force

The path of development often is accompanied by a shift in the population from rural to urban, in other words, from primary to secondary and tertiary sectors. Land resources being more or less fixed, the urbanisation of the economy releases human pressure on land with its high intensity of land-use and tends to provide greater physical acccess to social amenities. However, urbanisation also leads to its own set of environmental problems. The shift of population from rural to urban does not, necessarily imply a shift from agriculture to industry, but often results in a burgeoning tertiary sector that is considered as an indicator of disguised unemployment and underemployment of the population, particularly in the underdeveloped countries. Thus along with the level of urbanisation, it is necessary to include the strength of the industrial or secondary sector as a variable in measuring development.

The level of industrialisation as reflected by the percentage of the labour force in industry has, therefore, been selected as an additional variable to give weightage to the concept of an urbanised-industrialised economy. Thus the work force engaged in industry becomes an important complement to the level of urbanisation when gauging the level of development of an economy.

Per Capita Electricity Consumption

Standard of living of the population is positively associated with energy use. The sources of energy may be traditional and non-commercial (such as collected fuel wood, cow dung, etc.) or commercial (such as electricity, petroleum, coal, etc.). Thus, the consumption of electricity would reflect not only the level of industrialisation in a country, but also the availability of basic necessities like domestic lighting and the access to labour saving and effective domestic appliances. It could be taken as an effective indicator of quality of life.

Adult Literacy Rate

A literate population reflects the receptivity of the populace to new ideas, scientific methods and modern techniques. The level of nutrition, health, sanitation, modernisation of agriculture and industry are all highly correlated with the adult literacy rate.

Life Expectancy at Birth

Life expectancy at birth reflects the existing living conditions in terms of availability of food, drinking water, sanitation, housing, medical care. It is one of the most widely used indicators for assessing quality of life.

Infant Mortality Rate

Infant mortality rate reflects the level of pre-natal and post-natal care available in a country, the health and literacy level of the mother and in a broader sense, the attitudes and norms prevailing in society.

Population with Access to Safe Drinking Water

The supply of safe drinking water is, perhaps, the most significant preventive measure against water-borne disease. In most of the developing world, access to safe drinking water is still not ensured, particularly in the rural areas. The daily burden of trudging long distances to fetch water falls on the shoulders of the women and girl children adding to the already over heavy work load. Thus the proportion of the population with access to safe drinking water is a measure of both preventive health care and reduced workloads.

Population with Access to Sanitation

Similar to the availability of safe drinking water, access to sanitation also forms a major preventive health care measure. Sanitation, however, is a low priority item in most Asian countries and large segments of the population are still denied access to this basic infrastructure.

Daily Calorie Supply Per Capita

The right to freedom from hunger, while endorsed by all governments is still far from being realised. Daily calorie supply per capita, which is derived from the conversion of all food supplies in the country to calorific value divided by the population, indicates the availability of food within the country. It does not, however, reflect the access of the population to food. A comparison across countries of this variable would, however, indicate sustainability of a country with reference to food security.

Food Consumption as a Percentage of Total Household Consumption

While the daily calorie supply per capita indicates the supply of food within the country, the food consumption as a proportion of total household consumption reflects how accessible this food supply is to the people. It is a well documented fact that the poorer the household, the higher the proportion of its income that is expended on food. The increase in the proportion of food consumption down the ranks reflects both increasingly high prices of food items and the poverty levels of the population. The indicator would accordingly be negatively ranked.

Indicators of Quality of Environment

A set of environment related variables, numbering nine in all were selected for determining the quality of environment in the selected Asian countries. The indicators are listed below followed by a discussion on their relevance and limitations.

1. Per cent traditional fuel consumption to total household energy consumption (1993)
2. Per cent household energy from fuel wood (1990)
3. Per cent forest area to total land area (1993)
4. Per cent arable land to total land (1993)
5. Per cent irrigated land to arable land (1993)
6. Per cent annual rate of deforestation (1981–90)
7. Per cent annual rate of reforestation (1981–90)
8. Internal renewable water resources per capita (1995)
9. Per cent change in annual marine catch (1981–83 to 1991–93)
10. CO_2 emissions in metric tonnes per capita (1992)

Percentage Traditional Fuel Consumption to Total Energy Consumption

While most developed countries have managed a shift in their pattern of fuel consumption from traditional to non-traditional sources, the countries of Asia remain very largely dependent on traditional fuels. Research and development in non-conventional energy sources like wind, wave and solar energy continues, but large-scale use of these potential sources of energy remains limited. Only hydel and atomic power plants have been successful in the research for substitute fuels. A glance at the data recorded here reveals that of the nine countries for which data is available, only China and Thailand meet over 90 per cent of their demand through non-traditional fuels. India and Pakistan are dependent on traditional fuels to supply over 75 per cent of their demand. In fact, a country like Nepal meets 92 per cent of its fuel demand from traditional fuel sources. While all sources of energy have some environmental implications, in this analysis, it is posited that traditional sources, particularly fuel wood, have negative impact on the forest resources in particular and larger implications for the environment in general—notwithstanding the fact that modern-commercial sources of energy have enormous pollution implications including the risk factor involved in nuclear sources.

Percentage Household Energy from Fuel Wood

Fire wood consumption for household energy requirement is undeniably one of the major factors contributing to deforestation. With the growing demand for energy, the fluctuating supply and increasing prices of commercial fuel, and low income levels, the pressure on forests continues to grow, particularly in the South Asian Region. Large tracts of denuded forestland, specifically in the hill regions bear witness to this rampant environmental degradation.

In the tropical countries of Asia, the demand for fuel multiplies several folds in the mountain regions as lower temperatures necessitate fuel supply for heating as well as cooking. A case study of firewood requirements in the Kulu district of Himachal Pradesh places the demand at lying between 16 to 30 kg of firewood per household per day at altitudes of about 1800 m and between 30 to 100 kg of firewood per household per day at heights of 2300 m in summer and winter respectively (Maitra, 1992).

Attempts have been made, in India to offset this demand by supplying rationed kerosene oil at subsidised rates through fair price shops all over the country. Several rural development programmes have also focused on the introduction of more efficient cookers, solar cookers and bio-gas plants in an attempt to reduce this dependence. However, even in urban areas, there remains a fairly large segment of the lower and lower-middle income groups who still rely on traditional fuels. In India, in particular, traditional fuels include not only firewood, but also cow dung cakes. The extensive use of cow dung cakes as fuel in rural areas has resulted in the large-scale deprivation of one of the best sources of manure for agricultural fields and kitchen gardens. Thus, the usage of both wood and cow dung is a measure of the unsustainable use of natural resources and in the final reckoning, an indicator of environmental degradation.

It is worth noting that the first two indicators do not necessarily move together. For example, the percentage of traditional fuel consumption to total energy consumption, in the case of China is only 6 per cent whereas in the case of household energy, 80 per cent of the demand is met from fuel wood. A similar proportion of about 80 to 86 per cent can be observed in all the countries for which data is available.

Percentage Forest Area to Total Land Area

While the two previous indicators denote the on-going practices in energy use that affect forest resources, the percentage of forest area in a country is good indicator of the extent of virgin land available, the level of bio-diversity, the timber reserves and the non-timber forest produce available. In terms of forest area, the selected Asian countries range from the heavily forested countries of Malaysia and Bhutan to the almost totally barren Kuwait and Saudi Arabia. The norm of total land area required to be retained under forest cover is generally accepted as being around 30 per cent. With reference to this norm, seven of the twelve countries being studied fall below the minimum requirements. China, Bangladesh and Pakistan record particularly low levels of forested area.

Annual Rate of Deforestation (1981–90)

The rate of deforestation averaged over a decade is a good indicator of the Government's policy to control the devastation of the natural environment. As can be seen from the recorded values, every country in the region appears to have recorded negative rates of deforestation, with the exception of Bangladesh which still exhibits an extremely rapid rate of deforestation, as high as 11 per cent per annum.

Percentage Annual Rate of Reforestation (1981-90)

The percentage rate of reforestation averaged over the same decade would reflect government efforts at rejuvenating the natural forest wealth of the country. This ranges from as little as 3 per cent per annum in the case of Pakistan and Bangladesh to as much as over 30 per cent in the case of India, Nepal and Malaysia.

Taken in conjunction with the previous indicator, it would help reveal the survival rate of the replantation efforts, or in other words, the extent to which deforestation continues to be rampant. Take, for example, India, which has a reforestation rate of 32 per cent per annum, yet records an annual rate of deforestation which is –0.6 per cent. The implication is that all reforestation efforts have managed to barely offset the extent of deforestation taking place. In the case of Pakistan the actual increase in forest area is very close to the annual rate of reforestation i.e. 2.9 per cent as against 3 per cent.

Percentage Arable Land to Total Land Area

The extent of arable land in a country is a simple measure of the country's self-sufficiency in food crops or commercial crops which can be used to purchase food. It also indicates the utilisation of land and the efforts of the country to protect its land from degradation or to reclaim existing wasteland. In an acceptable proportion and in combination with agricultural productivity it can be taken as a positive indicator of the quality of the environment.

Percentage Irrigated Land to Arable Land

The proportion of arable land which enjoys assured water supply is indicative of the intensity of agriculture in a country. Irrigated land implies multiple cropping, high yielding varieties and, consequently, greater productivity, and intensive use of land resources. Taken in conjunction with the previous indicator, i.e. the percentage of arable land to total land area, it becomes obvious that countries like Pakistan, China and Sri Lanka which have only a small proportion of arable land to their total land area, tend to have a high intensity of irrigation to boost their output, whereas countries like India and Bangladesh with over 50 per cent of their land area classed as arable, record lesser proportion of irrigated land – only about one-third of their arable land is irrigated.

Internal Renewable Water Resources Per Capita

The availability of water is a critical indicator of both quality of life and environmental quality. Water resources hold the key to sustainable development. They also tend to reflect the health of the environment–the cycle of adequate forest cover, sufficient rainfall, moisture retention capacities and the availability of renewable water resources being an established one. The range of per capita renewable water resources is from an extremely high 58,000 cu. metres per capita per year in Bhutan to an average of between 2 to 3 cu. metres per capita per year in most of the Asian countries being studied.

Percentage Change in Annual Marine Catch (1981-83 to 1991-93)

While this indicator applies only to those countries with access to the ocean, it reflects both sustainability of food resources and exportable surplus. The increasing pressure on agricultural land and the demand for food lead to increasing exploitation of marine resources. Sharp increases in marine catch in a short period of time could be taken as a sign of unsustainable practices. Eight of the nine countries being studied indicated positive change ranging from a mere 4 per cent (Sri Lanka) to as much as 168 per cent in China. Only Malaysia reflects negative growth, as much as 13 per cent.

Per Capita Carbon Dioxide Emissions

In terms of air pollution, the choking of the lower atmosphere with noxious fumes creating health hazards as well as the green house effect and global warming, the role of CO_2 emissions is well known. As an indicator of quality of environment, this could well be the most reflective. Worked out in per capita terms, the values represent country averages, but of course, differences within the country would be considerable, particularly between urban and rural environments. Values range from 0.1 metric tonne per capita in Nepal to as high as 11.2 metric tonnes per capita in Kuwait and 13.1 metric tonnes per capita in Saudi Arabia. India records nine times as much as Nepal averaging 0.9 metric tonnes per capita.

Data Base

Data on the above indicators was collected for twelve Asian countries* including India. Data sources include the Human

* Bangladesh, Bhutan, China, India, Indonesia, Kuwait, Malaysia, Nepal, Pakistan, Saudi Arabia, Sri Lanka and Thailand.

Development Reports of the UNDP and the World Development Reports of the World Bank supplemented by other sources such as 'World Resources' of the World Resources Institute. For details see Appendix on Data Sources.

Composite Index

Sophisticated methods of constructing composite indices require sensitive and refined data sets. Given that the data are national aggregates, derived from various sources, and differences exist in the definition of variables in different countries, the method used for constructing a composite index must be simple, rather than sophisticated. This consideration suggested a simple ranking of the countries when the analysis deals with cross country comparisons, ranking of different States or sub-units when the analysis pertains to intra-country comparisons.

The two sets of indicators reflecting Quality Of Life (QOL) and Quality Of Environment (QOE) are collapsed into two composite indices. The technique adopted is a simple one based on the rank allotted to each country with reference to the ranks obtained by the other countries vis-a-vis each indicator e.g. the total number of observations or countries being twelve, the ranks range from one to twelve. In the case of data not being available for any country, the country in question is excluded from the ranking.

The country obtaining the highest score is ranked as one. If two or more countries have the same value, the same rank is given to each of them, then averaged by dividing by two or *'n'* as the case may be. The rank allotted to the next country in order of value then be given on the basis of the number of ranks already allotted e.g. Taking the quality of environment indicator 6, i.e. percentage annual rate of deforestation, both Pakistan and Thailand record the same value of –2.9 per cent which is the highest score. As the ranks to be allotted to the first and second countries are 1 and 2, the average score i.e.

$$\frac{1 + 2}{2}$$

is allocated to each of the two countries. The country coming next in order of merit is given rank 3, as both ranks 1 and 2 have already been allocated.

The same method of ranking is applied to each indicator following which, a composite index is obtained by adding the ranks scored by each country for all the indicators in question (10 indicators for the quality of environment index and 11 indicators for the Quality of Life Index). As it is difficult to obtain data on each indicator for every country, the composite scores are adjusted according to the number of variables included for each country. The final values obtained thus comprise two sets of ranks obtained by each country, one with reference to the quality of life, the other with reference to the quality of the environment (Table 2.3).

TABLE 2.3: **India and other Asian Countries : Composite Index**

		Composite			Composite	
	Country	Index QOL	Rank	Country	1994 Index QOE	Rank
		1			2	
1	Bangladesh	8.59	10	Bangladesh	6.15	9
2	Bhutan	10.11	11	Bhutan	6.21	10
3	China	5.91	6	China	5.8	8
4	India	7.41	9	India	5.55	5.5
5	Indonesia	6.04	7	Indonesia	5.55	5.5
6	Kuwait	1.87	1	Kuwait	9.33	12
7	Malaysia	2.7	2	Malaysia	5.25	4
8	Nepal	10.91	12	Nepal	4.61	2
9	Pakistan	7.14	8	Pakistan	4.3	1
10	Saudi Arabia	3.4	3	Saudi Arabia	9	11
11	Sri Lanka	5.54	5	Sri Lanka	5.7	7
12	Thailand	5.14	4	Thailand	4.94	3

Index of Sustainable Development

This section attempts to arrive at a single index of sustainable development by combining the two indices of QOL and QOE, by adding the composite scores and ranking the countries on this basis. The indicator thus derived remains a relative value which can be used only for purposes of comparative analysis and does not in any way represent the status of sustainable development. The relative positions of the twelve countries are recorded in Table 2.4. Malaysia not only emerges as the first ranking country among the twelve countries, but also the gap in the scores between the first and the second ranking country (Thailand) is substantial. Bhutan and Nepal rank the lowest. India stands ninth on the scale among the twelve countries. Since both the dimensions are equally weighted, high scores on one of the two affects the ranking. Thus, Kuwait by virtue of having a high QOL emerges as the third ranking country despite low scorès on QOE. It is, therefore, necessary to compare the countries along both the scales.

TABLE 2.4: **Index of Sustainable Development – Selected Asian Countries**

Country	Composite Index of Sustainable Development	Rank
Malaysia	7.95	1
Thailand	10.08	2
Kuwait	11.2	3
Sri Lanka	11.24	4
Pakistan	11.44	5
Indonesia	11.59	6
China	11.71	7
Saudi Arabia	12.4	8
India	12.96	9
Bangladesh	14.74	10
Nepal	15.52	11
Bhutan	16.32	12

Graphical Comparisons

To facilitate inter-country comparisons, a simple scatter graph can be used. The ranks on quality of life of each country were plotted against the rank on quality of environment. A study of the graph

(Fig.2.1) reveals the relative positions of the 12 selected countries with reference to status of quality of life of the population and the status of the environment.

India emerges in a medium position with reference to the state of the environment, but remains low in terms of quality of life. Malaysia and Thailand rank high in terms of both quality of life and quality of environment with Thailand having the edge over Malaysia in terms of environmental quality and Malaysia scoring higher on quality of life. China, Sri Lanka and Indonesia rank medium on both counts. Kuwait and Saudi Arabia, as expected, score highest in terms of quality of life, but remain extremely vulnerable in terms of status of environment. Bhutan and Bangladesh lag behind both environmentally and in terms of living conditions. Nepal and Pakistan rank fairly high as regards environmental quality, but score dismally low where quality of life is concerned. The spatial distribution of quality of life and quality of environment scores can be seen in Fig.2.2.

Quality of Life and Status of Environment—Trends in India (1951 to 1996)

When the analysis is restricted to India, the choice of variables is slightly wider. However, expanding the scope of analysis to over four decades poses restrictions of availability of data. Data was collected on a large number of variables annually for the period 1951 to 1996. However, gaps in the data restricted the variables to 28 with 15 indicators representing quality of life and 13 indicators representing status of the environment (See Tables 2.5 and 2.6).

One of the major problems encountered in dealing with aggregate time series data gathered at national, State and district level is the consistency – almost all positive indicators show positive trends and negative indicators show negative trends – which raises the question of reliability and credibility of the data base itself. This is particularly frustrating with reference to environmental dimensions, as major variables such as area under forest or pasture or crop land or area under foodgrain – all show steady increase. However, when expressed as ratios with reference to appropriate denominators – forest land in terms of forest area (in hectares) per person or pasture in terms of livestock per hectare—some meaningful trends emerge.

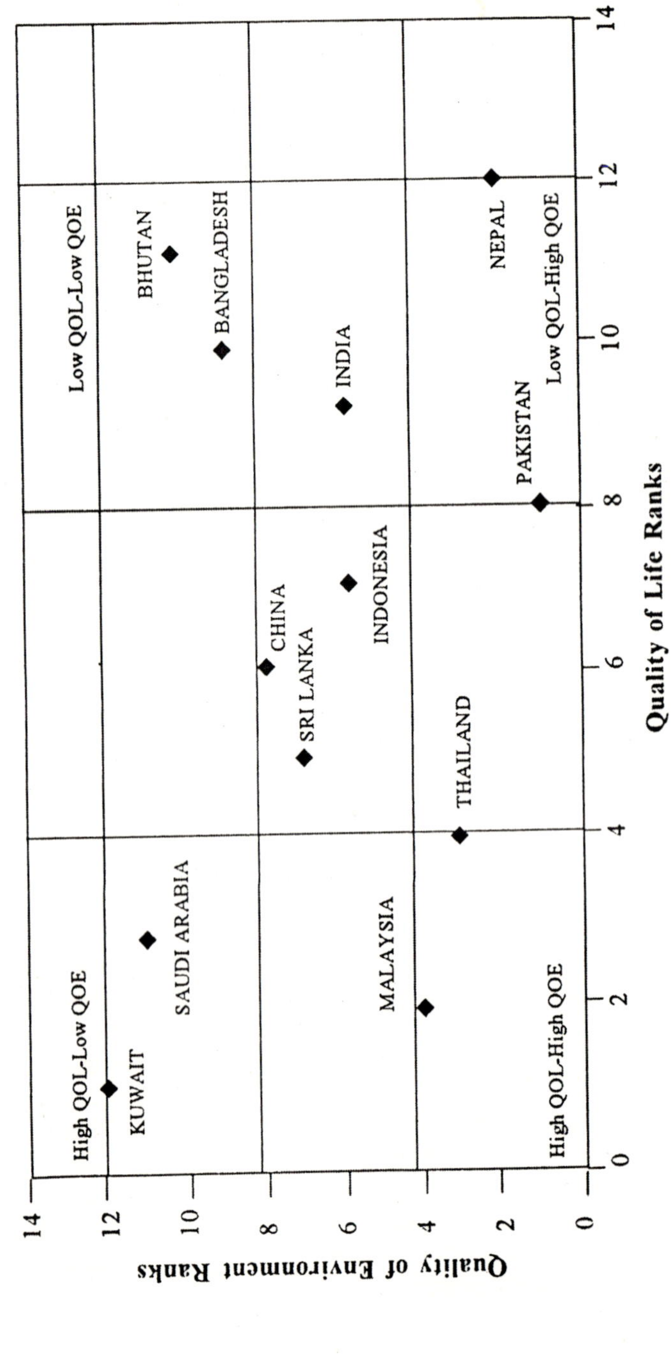

Fig. 2.1: Asia: Levels of Quality of Life and Quality of Environment

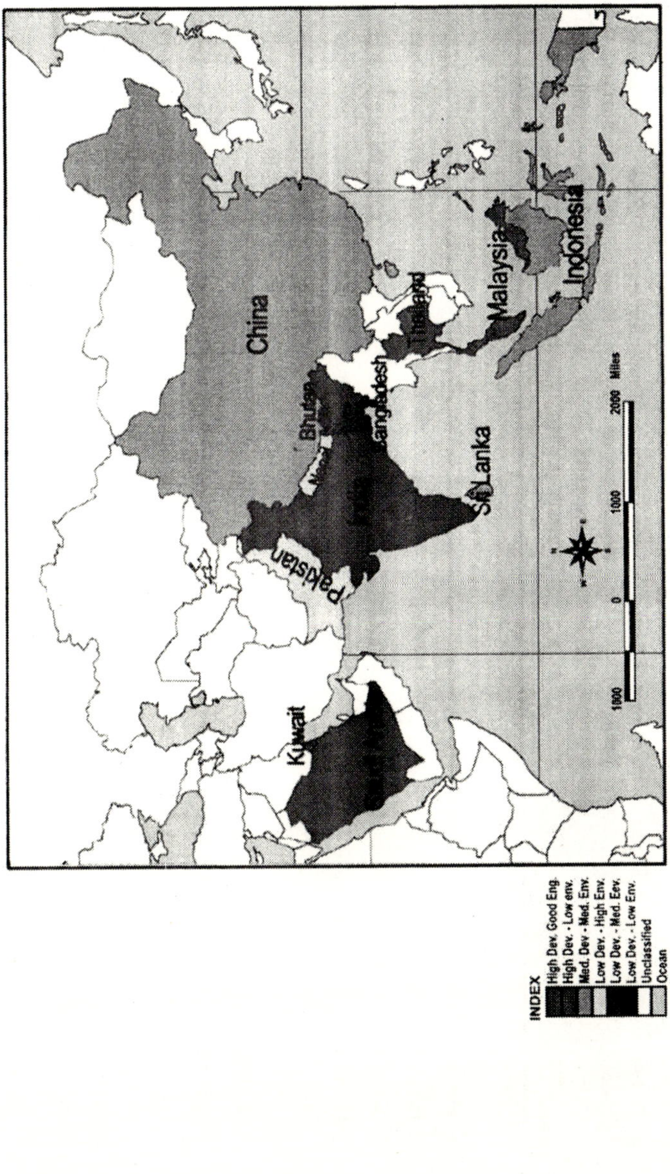

Fig. 2.2 : Asia : Relative Levels of Quality of Life and Quality of Environment

TABLE 2.5: India: Quality of Life Indicators 1951-1996

Year	Per Capita NNP	Rank	Reverse Rank	Year	Per Capita Availability of Electricity Domestic (kWh)	Rank	Reverse Rank	Year	Length of Surfaced Roads ('000 km.)	Rank	Reverse Rank
	1				2				3		
1995-96	9678.4	1	10	1990-91	38.2	1	8	1990-91	1001	1	8
1990-91	4983	2	9	1985-86	22.9	2	7	1985-86	825	2	7
1985-86	2730.2	3	8	1980-81	13.5	3	6	1980-81	684	3	6
1980-81	1630.1	4	7	1975-76	9.7	4	5	1970-71	398	4	5
1975-76	1064.6	5	6	1970-71	7	5	4	1960-61	263	5	4
1970-71	674.7	6	5	1965-66	4.8	6	3	1965-66	262	6	3
1965-66	458.7	7	4	1960-61	3.4	7	2	1955-56	183	7	2
1960-61	328.2	8	3	1955-56	2.4	8	1	1950-51	157	8	1
1950-51	238.8	9	2	1950-51				1975-76			
1955-56	233.1	10	1	1995-96				1995-96			

(*Contd.*)

TABLE 2.5: (Contd.)

Year	Persons per Hospital Bed	Rank	Reverse Rank	Year	Urban Population	Rank	Reverse Rank	Year	Life Expectancy at Birth	Rank	Reverse Rank
	4				5				6		
1990-91	1020.427724	1	7	1990-91	834650	1	5	1995-96	62.4	1	6
1980-81	1208.965838	2	6	1980-81	569495	2	4	1990-91	59.4	2	5
1970-71	1581.219257	3	5	1970-71	348655	3	3	1980-81	50.4	3	4
1960-61	1923.478261	4	4	1960-61	230000	4	2	1970-71	45.6	4	3
1965-66	1977.459016	5	3	1950-51	117178	5	1	1960-61	41.3	5	2
1955-56	2482.165605	6	2	1955-56				1950-51	32.1	6	1
1950-51	3099.557937	7	1	1965-66				1955-56			
1975-76	#DIV/O!			1975-76				1965-66			
1985-86	#DIV/O!	•		1985-86				1975-76			
1995-96				1995-96				1985-86			

(Contd.)

TABLE 2.5: *(Contd.)*

Year	Sex Ratio	Rank	Reverse Rank	Year	Infant Mortality Rate per '000 live births	Rank	Reverse Rank	Year	Literacy Rate	Rank	Reverse Rank
	7				8				9		
1950-51	947	1	5	1995-96	72	1	7	1990-91	52.2	1	5
1960-61	941	2	4	1990-91	80	2	6	1980-81	43.6	2	4
1980-81	936	3	3	1985-86	96	3	5	1970-71	34.5	3	3
1970-71	930	4	2	1980-81	110	4	4	1960-61	28.3	4	2
1990-91	928	5	1	1970-71	129	5	3	1950-51	18.3	5	1
1955-56				1950-51	146	6.5	1.5	1955-56			
1965-66				1960-61	146	6.5	1.5	1955-66			
1975-76				1955-56				1975-76			
1985-86				1965-66				1985-86			
1995-96				1975-76				1995-96			

(Contd.)

TABLE 2.5: *(Contd.)*

Year	Female Literacy Rate	Rank	Reverse Rank	Year	Availability of Milk in kg. per capita per day	Rank	Reverse Rank	Year	Availability of eggs per capita per day	Rank	Reverse Rank
	10				11				12		
1990-91	39.3	1	5	1995-96	0.197702937	1	7	1995-96	0.081578633	1	7
1980-81	29.75	2	4	1990-91	0.173384094	2	6	1990-91	0.067877139	2	6
1970-71	21.97	3	3	1985-86	0.160644916	3	5	1985-86	0.058883664	3	5
1960-61	15.34	4	2	1950-51	0.128236075	4	4	1980-81	0.040031436	4	4
1950-51	8.86	5	1	1980-81	0.125744869	5	3	1970-71	0.030672209	5	3
1955-56				1960-61	0.123857415	6	2	1960-61	0.017841661	6	2
1965-66				1970-71	0.109330623	7	1	1950-51	0.013819323	7	1
1975-76				1955-56	0			1955-56	0		
1985-86				1965-66	0			1965-66	0		
1995-96				1975-76	0			1975-76	0		

(Contd.)

TABLE 2.5: *(Contd.)*

Year	Availability of Fish in gms per capita per day	Rank	Reverse Rank	Year	Per Capita Net Availability of Pulses Per Day	Rank	Reverse Rank	Year	Per Capita Net Availability of Cereals per day in gms	Rank	Reverse Rank
	13				14				15		
1995-96	14.80229706	1	7	1990-91	12.9	1	10	1995-96	154	1	10
1990-91	13.37212762	2	6	1985-86	12.3	2	9	1990-91	145.7	2	9
1985-86	10.50033589	3	5	1975-76	11.4	3	8	1985-86	121.5	3	8
1980-81	9.717372489	4	4	1995-96	11.2	4	7	1980-81	104.8	4	7
1970-71	8.726571566	5	3	1960-61	11.1	5	6	1975-76	84.4	5	6
1960-61	7.18373009	6	2	1970-71	10.3	6	5	1970-71	84	6	5
1950-51	5.672560497	7	1	1955-56	10.2	7	4	1965-66	64.8	7	4
1955-56	0			1980-81	9.4	8	3	1960-61	64.6	8	3
1965-66	0			1965-66	8.7	9	2	1955-56	52.4	9	2
1975-76	0			1950-51	8	10	1	1950-51	44.3	10	1

TABLE 2.6: **India: Quality of Environment Indicators 1951-1996**

Year	Forest area per person (ha)	Rank	Reverse Rank	Year	Livestock per ha of pasture	Rank	Reverse Rank	Year	Rural Population per ha. of NSA	Rank	Reverse Rank
	1				2				3		
1955-56	1317.50064	1	9	1965-66	2323.504	1	8	1955-56	2.48732	1	9
1965-66	1275.50259	2	8	1960-61	2408.936	2	7	1950-51	2.52031	2	8
1960-61	1221.79024	3	7	1970-71	2664.289	3	6	1960-61	2.71686	3	7
1970-71	1159.3869	4	6	1955-56	2672.492	4	5	1965-66	2.89783	4	6
1950-51	1114.59251	5	5	1975-76	2927.402	5	4	1970-71	3.12491	5	5
1975-76	1108.4507	6	4	1980-81	3494.237	6	3	1975-76	3.38616	6	4
1980-81	979.244735	7	3	1985-86	3710.115	7	2	1980-81	3.7451	7	3
1985-86	893.403518	8	2	1950-51	4386.277	8	1	1985-86	4.06292	8	2
1990-91	797.874839	9	1	1990-91				1990-91	4.4491	9	1
1995-96				1995-96				1995-96			

(*Contd.*)

TABLE 2.6: *(Contd.)*

Year	Cropping Intensity	Rank	Reverse Rank	Year	Yield of Foodgrains (kg/ha)	Rank	Reverse Rank	Year	Area under Cereals (mil. ha)	Rank	Reverse Rank
	4				5				6		
1985-86	0.27	1	8	1995-96	1499	1	10	1980-81	104.2	1	9
1980-81	0.23	2	7	1990-91	1380	2	9	1975-76	103.7	2	8
1975-76	0.2	3	6	1985-86	1175	3	8	1985-86	103.6	3	7
1960-61	0.15	4	5	1980-81	1023	4	7	1990-91	103.2	4	6
1955-56	0.14	5	4	1975-76	944	5	6	1970-71	101.8	5	5
1965-66	0.14	6	3	1970-71	872	6	5	1995-96	98.7	6	4
1950-51	0.11	7	2	1960-61	710	7	4	1960-61	92	7	3
1970-71	0.07	8	1	1965-66	650	8	3	1955-56	87.3	8	2
1990-91				1955-56	610	9	2	1950-51	78.2	9	1
1995-96				1950-51	522	10	1	1965-66			

(Contd.)

TABLE 2.6: *(Contd.)*

Year	Area under Pulses (mil ha)	Rank	Reverse Rank	Year	Firewood Prod. (000 cu.m)	Rank	Reverse Rank	Year	Pulp and Match wood Prod. (000 cu. m)	Rank	Reverse Rank
	7				8				9		
1990-91	24.7	1	9	1950-51	10710	1	6	1950-51	3982	1	6
1975-76	24.45	2	8	1955-56	10810	2	5	1955-56	4158	2	5
1985-86	24.4	3	7	1960-61	11642	3	4	1960-61	5426	3	4
1960-61	23.6	4	6	1970-71	12090	4	3	1965-66	6395	4	3
1970-71	22.6	5	5	1965-66	13619	5	2	1970-71	9655	5	2
1980-81	22.5	6	4	1975-76	15122	6	1	1975-76	10772	6	1
1995-96	22.3	7	3	1980-81				1980-81			
1955-56	20.2	8	2	1985-86				1985-86			
1950-51	19.1	9	1	1990-91				1990-91			
1965-66				1995-96				1995-96			

(Contd.)

TABLE 2.6: *(Contd.)*

Year	Coal incl. Lignite Prod. (mil. tonnes)	Rank	Reverse Rank	Year	Crude Oil Prod. (mil. tonnes)	Rank	Reverse Rank	Year	Ratio of GDP from Primary Sector to Secondary Sector	Rank	Reverse Rank	Year	Food-grain Area in ha. per Person	Rank	Reverse Rank
	10				11				12				13		
1950-51	32.8	1	7	1950-51	0.26	1	7	1995-96	0.94	1	10	1955-56	2.8355145	1	9
1960-61	55.7	2	6	1960-61	0.45	2	6	1990-91	1.17	2	9	1950-51	2.679543	2	8
1970-71	76.3	3	5	1970-71	6.8	3	5	1985-86	1.4	3	8	1960-61	2.6125904	3	7
1980-81	119	4	4	1980-81	10.5	4	4	1980-81	1.63	4	7	1965-66	2.3129534	4	6
1985-86	162.3	5	3	1985-86	30.2	5	3	1975-76	1.96	5	6	1970-71	2.254961	5	5
1990-91	225.5	6	2	1995-96	32.2	6	2	1965-66	1.97	6	5	1980-81	1.8397531	6	4
1995-96	292.3	7	1	1990-91	33	7	1	1970-71	2.05	7	4	1985-86	1.7060634	7	3
1955-56				1955-56				1960-61	2.78	8	3	1990-91	1.5009393	8	2
1965-66				1965-66				1955-56	3.23	9	2	1995-96	1.3366812	9	1
1975-76				1975-76				1950-51	3.75	10	1	1975-76			

The thirteen indicators selected for assessing the quality of the environment are classified under four heads: carrying capacities, land-use patterns, technological improvements and consumption of natural resources:

I.	Carrying Capacities	:	1. Livestock per hectare of pasture 2. Rural population per hectare of net sown area 3. Foodgrain area in hectares per person 4. Forest area in hectares per person
II.	Land-use pattern	:	1. Area under cereals 2. Area under pulses
III.	Technological Improvement	:	1. Cropping intensity 2. Yield of foodgrains 3. Ratio of GDP from Primary sector to GDP from secondary sector
IV.	Consumption of natural resources	:	1. Firewood production 2. Pulp and match wood production 3. Coal including lignite production 4. Crude oil production

Data Sources and Discussion of Selected Variables

Data was collected from a large number of published sources. The major sources are the Census of India, Economic Survey, World Development Reports of the World Bank, etc. pertaining to different time periods (Detailed references are listed in Appendix on Data Sources).

Livestock Per Hectare of Pasture

The concept of carrying capacity or the ability of the natural environment to support a certain population, either human or animal, is basic to the assessment of sustainability. In terms of livestock, the country has been witnessing a steady increase in numbers, though not in quality. With ever increasing pressure on the available grazing grounds, the result has been increasing deterioration of pastures, inroads into forest land by livestock with resultant stripping of shrubs, bushes, the bark of trees and ultimately destruction of vegetation, and in semi-arid areas, the rapid increase of desertification. Many hold responsible the proliferation of small ruminants like sheep and goats, which tend to uproot grasses and shrubs and permanently destroy vegetative cover, rather than cattle for this rampant destruction. Government schemes for rural development in the sixties and seventies encouraged the breeding of these animals, as an additional source of income, without estimating the possible environmental impact. However, current policy aims at reducing the number of animals, substituting higher milk and meat yielding hybrids and encouraging stall feeding in an attempt at preventing further environmental degradation.

Rural Population Per Hectare of Net Sown Area

In a predominantly agricultural country like India, the dependence of almost three-quarters of the population on available cropland is obvious. The sharply reduced availability of cropland per rural person reflects the inability of the agricultural environment to provide a living to the rural population. Changing distribution of land holding by size classes of land, could perhaps, be a better indicator. However, even a less sharp indicator such as rural population per hectare of sown area reveals an increase of 1.8 times in the number of rural people per hectare of net sown area, despite increase in the net sown area of about 2300 million hectares over the same period (1951-91). This indicator would also reflect the rural out-migration and the consequent increase in the slum population of the large metropolises.

Area under Foodgrain (hectares per person)

Area under foodgrain per person mirrors the extent of the country's self sufficiency in food production as well as indicates the health of the land or its capability to produce the basic requirement of foodgrain. The fact that from the early fifties when foodgrain area was about 3 hectares per capita to the current position (mid-nineties) of about 1 hectare per person speaks for itself both in terms of population growth and in terms of changes in land-use patterns.

Area under Forest (hectares per person)

As published data on forest area records a steady increase over the past five decades, it was realised that aggregated data at country level in terms of area under forests did not reflect the large scale deforestation, change in forest canopy or actual condition of existing forests. Thus it was felt that a per capita value may be more truly representative of the true status vis-a-vis forests. The data reveals that the forest area per person has almost halved over the period in question. While norms in terms of forest area per person are not readily available, the change in per capita status does reflect the reducing forest cover.

Area under Cereals

The two indicators: area under cereals and area under pulses reflect the changing agricultural land-use pattern from the early fifties to the current period. From the sustainability point of view, area under foodgrains becomes a major determinant of sustainable land-use.

The data reveals a steadily increasing trend in area under cereals till the mid-eighties reflecting the country's policy objective of attaining self-sufficiency in food. However, in the five-year period from the mid-eighties to the nineties, there has been a slight fall in acreage to the extent of about 400,000 hectares.

Area under Pulses

In a country like India, where pulses form the major protein supplement to the diet, the production of and area under pulses form important indicators of human carrying capacity. Again, like the area under cereals, the area under pulses shows steady gains over the four decades till 1990-91. However, the last five year period from the early to the mid-nineties records a loss of as much as 2.4 million hectares of land under pulses. Coupled with the corresponding loss in area under cereals during the same period, it once again raises the issue of sustainability of food production.

Cropping Intensity

The next three indicators are all reflections of the level of technological improvement which would also imply more sustainable resource use and improved environmental quality.

Cropping intensity would indicate the ability of the land to produce a larger output for the same cropped area. The data reveals steady improvement for the period 1950-51 to 1985-86, except for a fall in cropping intensity in 1970-71. However, data for the nineties is not available, so that current trends cannot be assessed.

Yield of Foodgrains

India still ranks far below other developing countries in terms of foodgrain yields. A steadily increasing yield would imply increasing sustainability in terms of meeting foodgrain demands in the future. The data reveals not only a constant increase in yields over the last five decades, but more importantly, a substantial increase by as much as three times. However, that the increase in yields is largely at the cost of much greater increase in inputs such as irrigation, fertilizers, pesticides, power, etc., some of which have environmental and equity implications.

Ratio of GDP from Primary Sector to GDP from Secondary Sector

The contribution to the gross domestic product from various sectors of the economy would indicate the dependence of the country's economy on a particular sector. In the case of India, which is primarily an agricultural country, it was decided to consider the GDP from two sectors – the primary or agricultural sector and the secondary or industrial sector. The ratio between the GDP from these sectors was computed to derive the values.

The data shows that in the early fifties, GDP from the primary sector was as much as 3.75 times the GDP from the secondary sector. By the early nineties, there was almost equal contribution from both sectors. In the mid–nineties, however, GDP contribution from the secondary sector had outstripped that from the primary sector indicating a lessening of dependence on land-based produce and transition to a more sustainable economic base.

Firewood Production

The production of firewood in the country is a direct reflection of the depleting forest resources, particularly when private and commercial firewood production is negligible. Firewood plantations while attempted, have not achieved any great degree of success. Despite attempts at providing substitute fuels, the continued dependence of the country on firewood is obvious from the constant increase in production from the fifties to the seventies. There is a lack of data on this variable after the mid-seventies.

Pulp and Matchwood Production

Pulp and matchwood production together with the production of firewood represent the extent of degradation of forestland. Between 1950-51 and 1975-76, pulp and matchwood production recorded a nearly three-fold increase. Lack of current data, however, makes it difficult to identify current trends.

Coal Production (including lignite)

Despite the introduction of other fuels, the dependence on coal as a major fuel for the domestic, industrial and transport (railway) sectors remains unchanged. The large scale depletion of this non-renewable energy resource makes the long term sustainability of our energy resources questionable. The production of coal has registered a ten-fold increase between 1951 and 1996 with production stepping up by 1.5 times as recently as the early nineties.

Crude Oil Production

The production of crude oil has registered a tremendous increase from the early fifties recording 127 times greater production in 1991 as compared to 1951. The same logic of the exhaustion of non-renewable natural resources applies here.

Quality of Life Indicators

The set of quality of life indicators collected for the country, at five yearly intervals from 1950–51 to 1995–96, number fifteen in all. The indicators here are more or less the same as the ones selected earlier for inter-country comparisons. Hence discussion about choice of indicators is restricted to new indicators only. The list of indicators is given below:

1. Per capita net national product
2. Per capita availability of domestic electricity (kWh)
3. Length of surfaced roads per '000 sq. kms.
4. Persons per hospital bed
5. Percent urban population
6. Life expectancy at birth
7. Sex-ratio
8. Infant mortality rate per '000 live births
9. Adult literacy rate
10. Female literacy rate
11. Availability of milk in kg per capita per day
12. Availability of eggs per capita per day
13. Availability of fish in gms per capita per day
14. Per capita net availability of pulses in gms per day
15. Per capita net availability of cereals in gms per day

Per Capita Availability of Domestic Electricity

While the corresponding variable selected for the country comparisons was per capita electricity consumption, for India, time series data on consumption of electricity was not available. Hence, the availability of domestic electricity was taken as a substitute variable. The sixteen fold increase in availability of domestic energy from the mid-fifties to the mid-nineties would indicate the improvement in the standard of living, and the utilisation of labour-saving and basic utility devices.

Persons Per Hospital Bed

In a country as large and populous as India, the provision of basic services including health services is a major challenge. Here, increase in physical numbers may not be a proper measure of availability. Hence, rather than taking the number of hospital beds available, the number of persons per hospital bed was computed. The position from 1950–51 to 1990–91 has improved by over three times. However, Indian norms of one hospital bed per 20C persons are still far from being met.

Sex Ratio

While the country has been registering rapid gains in terms of national income, power generation, literacy, health services, food production and the like, there still remains an area where development trends are being reversed in an almost inexplicable manner. Even at the national level, the sex ratio or the number of females per '000 males has been steadily falling. Implications in terms of illiteracy, ignorance, maternal and girl child health, and in the totality of gender equity and quality of life are obvious.

Female Literacy Rate

While the adult literacy rate has been selected as an indicator, it was felt that the female literacy rate, taken separately, would form a complementary indicator. It can be seen from the data, that while female literacy rates have recorded as much as a four fold increase over the four decades in question, the 1990-91 female literacy rate is still dismally low with not even half the female population being recorded as literates.

Indicators of Food Security

The next five indicators represent the food security aspect of the country's development. In the section on inter-country comparisons, the corresponding indicator was daily calorie supply per capita. Here, however, data was available on a number of essential food items covering both carbohydrate and protein requirements for basic nutrition.

Thus five simple indicators in the form of availability per day of cereals, pulses, milk, eggs and fish have been selected. It must, of course, be remembered that while these indicators reflect major strides in the country's production of these items, they do not reflect its distribution, or in other words, actual consumption by the people. Thus while the overall picture may have registered tremendous improvement, income disparities may still prevent access.

Availability of Milk Per Capita Per Day

The availability of milk has registered a roughly 1.5 times increase in 1995-96 over the base year 1950-51. Surprisingly, milk production fell from the early fifties till the early eighties from when there was a turning point and a steady growth was recorded.

Availability of Eggs Per Capita Per Day

In a predominantly vegetarian country, like India where meat does not form part of the regular diet, eggs have entered the daily diet as a major source of protein. The demand for eggs has registered a sharp increase and availability has grown correspondingly with eight times the number of eggs being available in per capita terms, despite the increase in population over four and a half decades.

Availability of Fish Per Capita Per Day

Fish could well fulfil the protein requirements of the future as a more sustainable substitute for meat. Animals reared for meat have implications for environmental sustainability in terms of fodder and feed requirements and the consequent increase in demand for pasture and crop acreage. Thus the availability of fish would indicate an alternative and more environment friendly source. The data reveals an increase of 2.6 times in the per capita availability of fish over the past four decades.

Per Capita Net Availability of Pulses Per Day

As mentioned in an earlier section, pulses are the most important source of protein in the Indian diet. In the section on quality of environment indicators, it was seen that area under pulses has begun to decline. Data on availability shows fluctuation with a generally rising availability from the early fifties, a sharp fall during the two decades between the mid-fifties to the mid-seventies, and then a steadily rising trend till 1995 – 96 which records a sudden shortfall of as much as 28 gms per capita per day.

Per Capita Net Availability of Cereals Per Day

The availability of cereals has registered a continuous growth with a spurt in output from the mid-seventies onwards reflecting the impact of the green revolution. From the early fifties a 3.5 times increase in per capita net availability has been recorded implying a substantial contribution to quality of life in the country.

Construction of Indices of Quality of Life and Status of Environment

The two sets of indicators representing quality of life and quality of environment were again aggregated to form a composite index for each dimension. As the intention, here, was to plot the scores obtained with regard to the two selected dimensions, in the form of linear graphs, the method of ranking was reversed. Thus, the observation recording the highest value with regard to a particular indicator was given the highest possible score e.g. where a total of ten values for ten observations were available, the observation recording the highest value obtains a score of ten. Once again, the total composite value obtained for each observation across the range for 15 indicators in the case of quality of environment were averaged by dividing by the number of indicators for which data was available (Table 2.7). The average composite score for each observation i.e. each year was then plotted on the graph (Fig. 2.3).

It can be seen from the graph that while the quality of life has registered substantial gains over the forty–five year period in question, the quality of the environment has remained more or less static with ups and downs within a range of 4.1 to 5.3. However, a definite downward trend is visible after 1976. After 1982, the focus seems to be totally on improving the quality of life, with the resultant impact being visible in the decline of the environmental status. However, it must be remembered that the trends brought out in the graph are only indicative, as some of the selected indicators are only crude reflections of environmental quality.

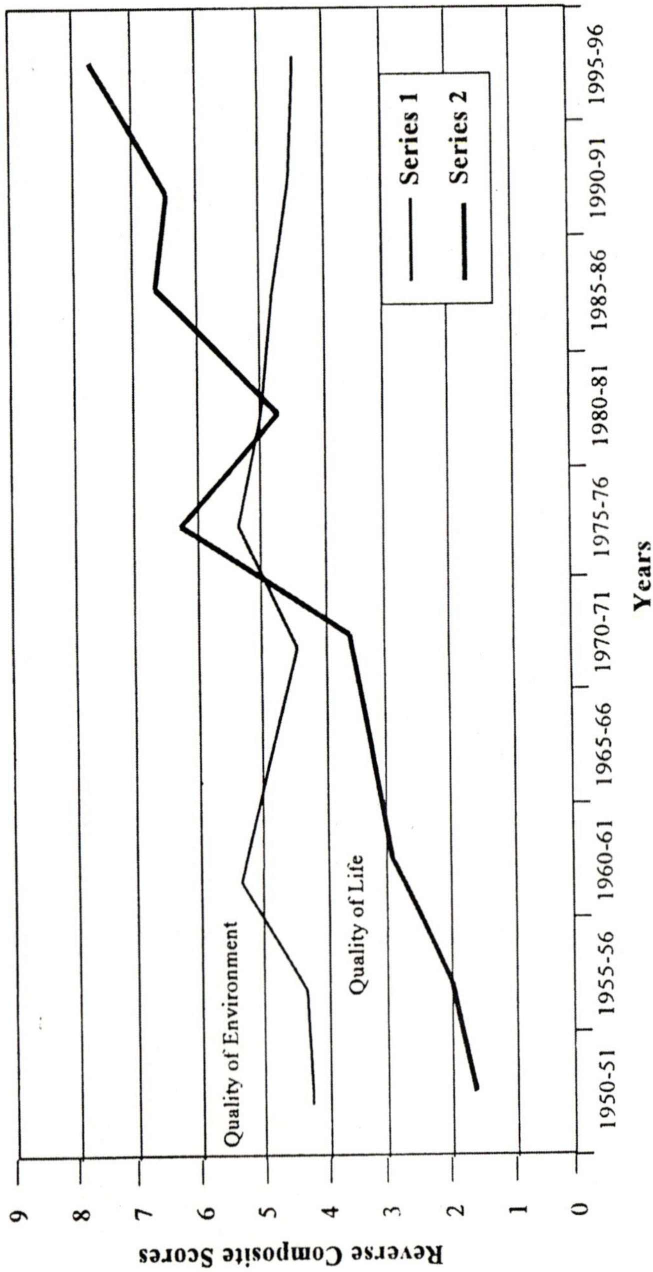

Fig. 2.3: India: Trends in Quality of Life and Quality of Environment

TABLE 2.7: **Composite Index of QOL and QOE (India: 1950-51 to 1995-96)**

Quality of Life Indicators		Quality of Environment Indicators	
Year	Reverse Score	Year	Reverse Score
1950-51	1.61	1950-51	4.15
1955-56	2.00	1955-56	4.19
1960-61	2.77	1960-61	5.31
1965-66	3.17	1965-66	4.89
1970-71	3.53	1970-71	4.38
1975-76	6.25	1975-76	5.30
1980-81	4.67	1980-81	5.00
1985-86	6.55	1985-86	4.82
1990-91	6.47	1990-91	4.55
1995-96	7.63	1995-96	4.43

During the decade 1973 to 1982, the ups and downs recorded, perhaps, reflect the changing policy priorities between environmental and developmental dimensions, with the developmental focus gaining greater priority from 1983 onwards as described above.

Strangely enough, prior to 1961, both the quality of life and the quality of environment scores are low, the implication being that low levels of development or lower rate of development does not necessarily imply a better environmental quality. Both the quality of life and the quality of the environment record substantial improvement in the decade 1951–1961. The next decade 1961–71 records a slight improvement in quality of life coupled with a sharp decline in the index of quality of environment.

The scatter gram plotted for the quality of life and quality of environment scores obtained by various South Asian countries in the earlier part of this chapter, was also repeated here with reference to specific points of time in the period 1951 – 96 (Table 2.8 and Fig. 2.4). The methodology followed was the same as earlier, i.e., with the highest value being ranked as 1.

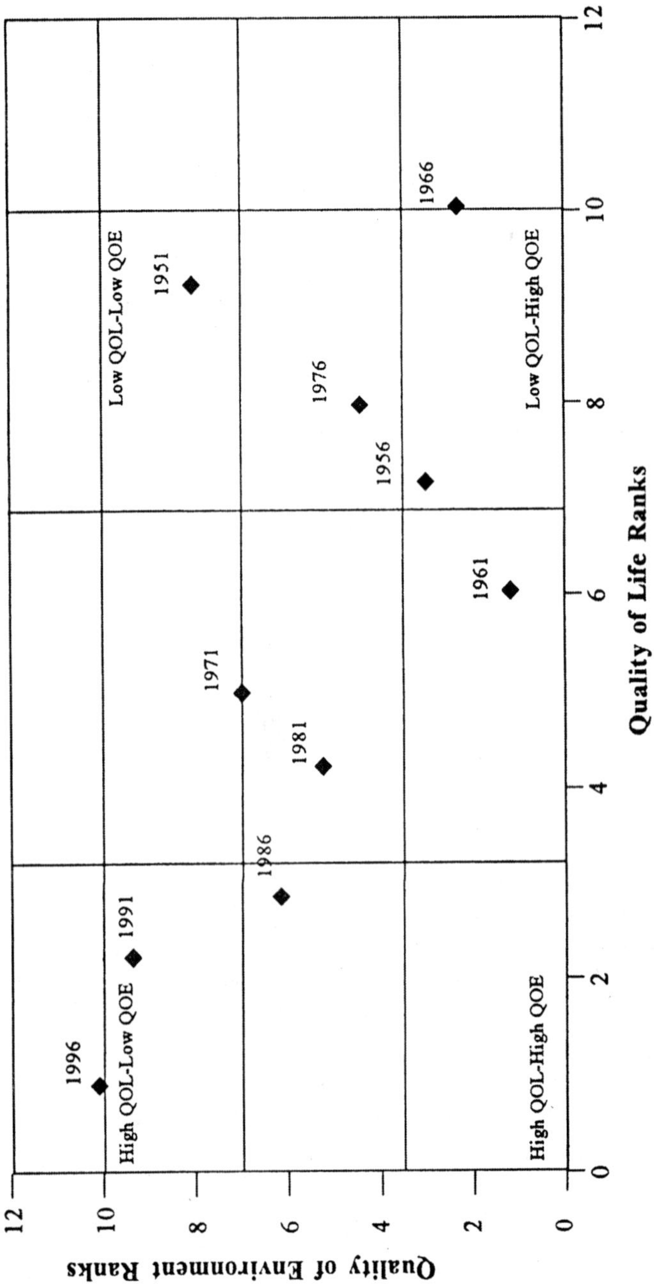

Fig. 2.4: India: Changes in Quality of Life and Environmental Status

TABLE 2.8: **India - Composite Scores**

Quality of Life Indicators			Quality of Environment Indicators		
Year	Composite Score	Rank	Year	Composite Score	Rank
1950-51	6.46	9	1950-51	5.80	8
1955-56	5.87	7	1955-56	4.54	3
1960-61	5.37	6	1960-61	2.46	1
1965-66	6.67	10	1965-66	4.44	2
1970-71	4.73	5	1970-71	4.85	7
1975-76	6.25	8	1975-76	4.60	4
1980-81	3.53	4	1980-81	4.64	5
1985-86	2.67	3	1985-86	4.82	6
1990-91	1.73	2	1990-91	5.33	9
1995-96	1.37	1	1995-96	5.57	10

The ranks obtained for each of the selected time periods were then summed across the variables to obtain a composite index. The composite value was then adjusted according to the number of variables for which data was available. The averaged composite index was then re-ranked with the lowest score being allotted the first rank and so forth. Thus two sets of final ranks are derived – one depicting the rank scored in each year with reference to the quality of life, the other representing the score on the status of environment.

The Nineties fall into the high development, poor environment category, from the mid fifties to the mid sixties in the low development, high environmental score category and the early fifties represent the period when both environmental quality and quality of life was poor. The years from the mid sixties through the eighties record the transition to greater weightage to economic development without necessarily ignoring environmental considerations.

3

QUALITY OF LIFE AND STATUS OF ENVIRONMENT
Inter-State Comparisons

This chapter attempts to classify fifteen* major States of the Indian Union on the basis of two sets of indicators – one relating to Quality of Life (QOL), the other to status of the environment, with a view to assessing the current level of each State in terms of sustainability. A comparison over time is also attempted to trace the trends in the two dimensions.

While the long standing debate between development and environment has resolved itself into a search for sustainable development, the concept of development itself has changed and broadened from a purely 'economic well-being' concept to a 'quality of life' concept. While a certain level of economic development is undisputedly essential to the quality of life, economic indicators alone do not capture the totality of QOL. Many attempts have been made at developing QOL indicators. Of these, perhaps the best known and simplest is the Human Development Index (HDI) of the United Nations. Measured on a scale of 0 to 1, it aggregates three indicators: longevity – life expectancy at birth, knowledge – literacy rates, and command over resources—per capita GDP adjusted to purchasing power. As these indicators are national averages, they do not reflect unequal distribution, but the inclusion of longevity and education does indirectly indicate individual access to health care, education and food. Country-wide comparisons reveal results which conflict with

* As data on several indicators was not available for the State of Himachal Pradesh and no data at all was available for Jammu & Kashmir, the two States were left out of the analysis and the study pertains to only fifteen States.

the traditional measures of income e.g. Sri Lanka with a per capita GDP of \$2053 has an HDI of 0.79, while Brazil with a GDP of \$4307 per capita has an HDI of 0.78 indicating a concentration of access to food and social services among the wealthier sections of the population.

While the HDI measures changes in human welfare, it ignores environmental degradation. As a result, increases in HDI may be made at the cost of depleting natural resources, thus implying unsustainability in the long run. This chapter attempts to offset these problems by deriving composite scores for each State on both QOL (Quality of Life) and QOE (Quality of Environment) indicators, thus identifying sustainable development paths.

Data Base and Methodology

The choice of State as a unit of analysis owes more to the availability of data rather than to homogeneity of physical attributes. However, as the State is an administrative unit, it also lends itself to the implementation of suggested norms or modifications of existing policy.

As mentioned above, the fifteen major States of the country for which comparative statistics are available, have been selected. Data has been collected on twenty-two variables from a variety of sources. While the major source of data is the Census of India, Statistical Abstracts, Statistical Diaries, the Economic Survey of India, etc. have been used to supplement the major data source, where necessary (see Appendix on Data Sources).

The twenty-two variables have been grouped into two sets: QOL indicators and QOE indicators (Table 3.1 and 3.2). Detailed below are the selected indicators and the reasons for selecting them.

Quality of Life (QOL) Indicators

The indicators selected for assessing the quality of life in each of the States number eleven in all.

1. *Per capita net State domestic product*
2. *Per capita consumption of electricity*
3. *Percentage of electrified villages to total inhabited villages*

TABLE 3.1: **Indian States 1991: Quality of Life Indicators**

Rank	State	Per capita net State domestic product (Rs.) 1991-92	Rank	State	Per capita Consumption of electricity (kWh) 1991-92	Rank	State	%age of electrified villages to total inhabited villages 1991-92	Rank	State	Length of total surfaced roads per 100 sq. km. of area 1988-89
	1			2			3			4	
1	Punjab	9713	1	Punjab	622	4	Andhra Pradesh	100	1	Kerala	103.5
2	Haryana	8722	2	Gujarat	507	4	Gujarat	100.0	2	Tamil Nadu	98
3	Maharashtra	7997	3	Haryana	480	4	Haryana	100.0	3	Punjab	83.8
4	Gujarat	6312	4	Maharashtra	432	4	Karnataka	100.0	4	Haryana	53.5
5	Karnataka	5898	5	Tamil Nadu	334	4	Kerala	100.0	5	Maharashtra	45.8
6	Tamil Nadu	5817	6	Karnataka	299	4	Maharashtra	100.0	6	Karnataka	45.5
7	West Bengal	5300	7	Orissa	298	4	Punjab	100.0	7	Gujarat	33.3
8	Andhra Pradesh	5220	8	Andhra Pradesh	288	8	Tamil Nadu	99.9	8	West Bengal	32.5
9	Kerala	4613	9	Madhya Pradesh	267	9	Assam	97.6	9	Uttar Pradesh	29.6
10	Assam	4594	10	Rajasthan	232	10	Madhya Pradesh	90.9	10	Andhra Pradesh	27.4
11	Rajasthan	4402	11	Kerala	198	11	Rajasthan	79.4	11	Bihar	17.5
12	Madhya Pradesh	4383	12	Uttar Pradesh	174	12	Uttar Pradesh	74.0	12	Madhya Pradesh	16.6
13	Uttar Pradesh	4001	13	West Bengal	151	13	West Bengal	73.7	13	Rajasthan	16.3
14	Orissa	3816	14	Bihar	115	14	Bihar	69.9	14	Assam	12.5
15	Bihar	2786	15	Assam	98	15	Orissa	69.8	15	Orissa	12.4

(Contd.)

TABLE 3.1: *(Contd.)*

Rank	State	Number of Beds per lakh population 1990	Rank	State	% Urban Population	Rank	State	Life Expectancy at Birth	Rank	State	Sex Ratio (Number of Females per thousand males)
	5			6			7			8	
1	Kerala	245	1	Maharashtra	38.7	1	Kerala	71.3	1	Kerala	1036
2	Maharashtra	146	2	Gujarat	34.5	2	Punjab	66.6	2	Tamil Nadu	974
3	Gujarat	124	3	Tamil Nadu	34.1	3	Maharashtra	63.4	3	Andhra Pradesh	972
4	Punjab	104	4	Karnataka	30.9	4	Haryana	62.5	4	Orissa	971
5	Tamil Nadu	88	5	Punjab	29.5	5	Karnataka	62.2	5	Karnataka	960
6	West Bengal	80	6	West Bengal	27.5	6	Tamil Nadu	61.5	6	Maharashtra	934
7	Karnataka	78	7	Andhra Pradesh	26.9	7	West Bengal	61.4	7	Gujarat	934
8	Assam	68	8	Kerala	26.4	8	Andhra Pradesh	60.2	8	Madhya Pradesh	931
9	Andhra Pradesh	56	9	Haryana	24.6	9	Gujarat	59.5	9	Assam	923
10	Rajasthan	53	10	Madhya Pradesh	23.2	10	Bihar	57.5	10	West Bengal	917
11	Orissa	45	11	Rajasthan	22.9	11	Rajasthan	56.3	11	Bihar	911
12	Haryana	43	12	Uttar Pradesh	19.8	12	Orissa	55.4	12	Rajasthan	910
13	Uttar Pradesh	38	13	Orissa	13.4	13	Uttar Pradesh	55.4	13	Punjab	882
14	Madhya Pradesh	34	14	Bihar	13.1	14	Asssam	54.1	14	Uttar Pradesh	879
15	Bihar	33	15	Assam	11.1	15	Madhya Pradesh	53.4	15	Haryana	865

(Contd.)

TABLE 3.1: *(Contd.)*

Rank	State	Rural Infant Mortality Rate per thousand 1991	Rank	State	% Female Literates
	9			10	
1	Kerala	17	1	Kerala	86.2
2	Punjab	58	2	Maharashtra	52.3
3	Tamil Nadu	65	3	Tamil Nadu	51.3
4	Maharashtra	69	4	Punjab	50.4
5	Bihar	71	5	Gujarat	48.6
6	Gujarat	73	6	West Bengal	45.6
7	Haryana	73	7	Karnataka	44.3
8	West Bengal	76	8	Assam	43
9	Andhra Pradesh	77	9	Haryana	40.5
10	Rajasthan	82	10	Orissa	34.7
11	Assam	83	11	Andhra Pradesh	32.7
12	Karnataka	87	12	Madhya Pradesh	28.8
13	Uttar Pradesh	97	13	Uttar Pradesh	25.3
14	Madhya Pradesh	131	14	Bihar	22.9
15	Orissa	131	15	Rajasthan	20.4

TABLE 3.2: **India States 1991: Quality of Environment Indicators**

Rank	State	% Growth in Forest Area	Rank	State	% Barren Land	Rank	State	% Pastures	Rank	State	% Tree Crops
	1			2			3			4	
1	Haryana	16	1	Rajasthan	0.2	1	Madhya Pradesh	6.3	1	Orissa	4.6
2	West Bengal	3.11	2	Punjab	1.5	2	Karnataka	6.1	2	Assam	3.1
3	Rajasthan	3.05	3.5	Kerala	2.1	3	Rajasthan	5.3	3.5	Karnataka	1.8
4	Gujarat	2.9	3.5	West Bengal	2.1	4	Maharashtra	5	3.5	Uttar Pradesh	1.8
5	Uttar Pradesh	1.06	5	Orissa	2.8	5	Orissa	4.6	5	Bihar	1.5
6	Karnataka	0.87	6.5	Haryana	3.6	6	Gujarat	4.5	6	Tamil Nadu	1.4
7	Kerala	0.43	6.5	Uttar Pradesh	3.6	7	Andhra Pradesh	3.2	7	Kerala	1.2
8	Punjab	0.34	8.5	Karnataka	4.2	8	Assam	2.3	8	Andhra Pradesh	1
9	Tamil Nadu	0.3	8.5	Tamil Nadu	4.2	9	Uttar Pradesh	1.2	9.5	Maharashtra	0.6
10	Orissa	-0.25	10	Madhya Pradesh	5.2	10	Tamil Nadu	1.1	9.5	West Bengal	0.6
11	Madhya Pradesh	-0.28	11	Maharashtra	5.6	11	Bihar	0.8	11	Madhya Pradesh	0.3
12	Andhra Pradesh	-0.37	12	Bihar	5.9	12	Haryana	0.6	12	Rajasthan	0.1
13	Bihar	-0.4	13	Andhra Pradesh	8.3	14	Kerala	0.1	14	Gujarat	0
14	Maharashtra	-0.46	14	Gujarat	14.2	14	Punjab	0.1	14	Haryana	0
15	Assam	-2.96	15	Assam	19.6	14	West Bengal	0.1	14	Punjab	0

(Contd.)

TABLE 3.2: *(Contd.)*

Rank	State	% Culturable Waste	Rank	State	% Current Fallow to NSA	Rank	State	% Area under Foodgrains to GCA	Rank	State	Cropping Intensity
	5			6			7			8	
1	Haryana	0.5	1	Andhra Pradesh	32	1.5	Bihar	89.9	1	Punjab	177.9
2	Punjab	0.8	2	Assam	32	1.5	Uttar Pradesh	80.3	2	Haryana	165.6
3	Assam	1.3	3	Tamil Nadu	26	2	Punjab	75.6	3	West Bengal	162.4
4	West Bengal	2	4	Bihar	25.2	3	West Bengal	75	4	Orissa	152.2
5	Bihar	2.3	5.5	Rajasthan	13.8	4	Madhya Pradesh	74.9	5	Uttar Pradesh	147.3
6	Tamil Nadu	2.3	5.5	Karnataka	10.7	5	Orissa	73.9	6	Assam	140.3
7	Karnataka	2.4	7	West Bengal	8.6	6	Assam	71.8	7	Bihar	136.1
8	Orissa	3	8	Gujarat	7.3	7	Haryana	68.9	8	Kerala	134.4
9	Andhra Pradesh	3.1	9	Uttar Pradesh	6.6	8	Maharashtra	66.1	9	Madhya Pradesh	122.1
10	Kerala	3.3	10.5	Madhya Pradesh	5.2	9	Rajasthan	65.3	10	Maharashtra	121.9
11	Maharashtra	3.3	10.5	Haryana	4.4	10.5	Karnataka	59.8	11	Andhra Pradesh	119.7
12	Uttar Pradesh	3.7	12	Orissa	4.4	10.5	Tamil Nadu	58.6	12	Tamil Nadu	118.9
13	Madhya Pradesh	3.8	12	Maharashtra	4	13	Andhra Pradesh	58	13	Rajasthan	118.3
14	Gujarat	10.4	14	Kerala	1.9	14	Gujarat	45.6	14	Karnataka	113.3
15	Rajasthan	16.8	15	Punjab	1.1	15	Kerala	19.5	15	Gujarat	111.5

(Contd.)

TABLE 3.2: *(Contd.)*

Rank	State	Yield of Food-grains (kg/ha)	Rank	State	Per Capita Availability of Food-grains	Rank	State	% Workers in Min. & Quarry.
	9			10			11	
1	Punjab	3392.5	1	Punjab	949.1	1	Punjab	0
2	Haryana	2344	2	Haryana	580.7	2.5	Haryana	0.1
3	Tamil Nadu	1914.5	3	Madhya Pradesh	271.9	2.5	Uttar Pradesh	0.1
4	Kerala	1883	4	Uttar Pradesh	256.4	4	Tamil Nadu	0.3
5	Uttar Pradesh	1742.4	5	Rajasthan	248.5	5.5	Gujarat	0.4
6	West Bengal	1735	6	Orissa	219.3	5.5	Maharashtra	0.4
7	Andhra Pradesh	1588.5	7	Andhra Pradesh	185.4	7	Assam	0.5
8	Bihar	1300.3	8	West Bengal	165.5	8	Karnataka	0.7
9	Assam	1262.2	9	Maharashtra	154.3	9	West Bengal	0.8
10	Gujarat	1024.1	10	Assam	153.6	10.5	Andhra Pradesh	0.9
11	Madhya Pradesh	1006	11	Kerala	152.7	10.5	Madhya Pradesh	0.9
12	Orissa	979.3	12	Karnataka	142.3	13	Kerala	1
13	Karnataka	909.5	13	Bihar	141.9	13	Orissa	1
14	Rajasthan	864	14	Tamil Nadu	133.1	13	Rajasthan	1
15	Maharashtra	843	15	Gujarat	117.2	15	Bihar	1.3

While this indicator would be partly reflected in the previous one, i.e. per capita consumption of electricity, it merits recognition as a separate indicator. In a country like India where 75 per cent of the population lives in rural areas, the real measure of development lies in assessing the rural areas. With the long stated objective of hundred percent rural electrification, it is worthwhile to assess just how far are the various States from achieving this objective.

4. *Length of total surfaced roads per 100 sq. km of area*

The surfaced road network in an area reflects the all-weather access of the local population to markets, medical and educational facilities as well as the opening up of the area to outside influence. It is thus a potent indicator of development. The conversion of road length into road density makes the indicator scale free.

5. *Number of beds in hospitals and dispensaries per unit population*

The number of hospital and dispensary beds reflects the level of health care available to the population. The indicator is made scale free by using the number of beds per 100,000 population.

6. *Percentage urban to total population*
7. *Life expectancy at birth*
8. *Sex ratio*
9. *Rural infant mortality rate*

Infant mortality rates mirror the general health and nutrition status not only of mothers, but the populace at large. They also reflect the availability of adequate medical facilities for both pre- and post-natal and paediatric care. The level of infant mortality in the urban and rural areas of the State taken together, is often distorted by the scores obtained by the urban segment. Rural infant mortality rates taken alone provide a clearer picture of the situation prevailing in the State and the reality faced by over 75 per cent of the population.

10. *Percentage female literates to total female population*
11. *Percentage of rural households getting two square meals a day*

The level of food security in a region is a basic indicator of economic development as well as of quality of life. As a measure of sheer poverty, no better indicator could be selected. In the Indian context, across all States, the level of food security is consistently higher in urban areas. As has often been emphasized, hunger in India stems more from lack of purchasing power, rather than actual shortfalls in availability of food. Better employment opportunities in urban areas could be the reason for the higher levels of food security. Thus rural food security in its most basic form of freedom from hunger has been selected as an indicator here. The data pertain to the years between 1988-89 to 1991-92. The exact time period for each indicator is given in Table 3.2.

Quality of Environment (QOE) Indicators

To assess the quality of the environment, a set of eleven indicators has been selected. These indicators reflect largely man's use of the environment, rather than the natural state of the environment in the region, e.g. instead of selecting the percentage of forest area to total area which may well be a function of natural factors like topography, climate and soil, the indicator selected is growth in forest area which may be positive or negative reflecting whether forest resources are being indiscriminately used as an economic resource or whether attempts have been made to make this resource use sustainable.

1. *Percentage growth in forest area*

As explained above the growth rate of area under forests reflects attempts at sustainable economic utilisation or regeneration of this natural resource. The ranks obtained by the various States show that States rich in forest resources like Assam and Madhya Pradesh record negative growth and States like Haryana, West Bengal and Rajasthan with low proportions of area under forest register positive growth.

2. *Percentage barren land to total reporting area*

The percentage of barren to total land would reflect both the natural landscape and man's attempts at reclamation. Surprisingly, a State like Rajasthan, characterised by deserts and droughts records only 0.2 percent of its land as barren.

3. *Percentage area under pastures to total reporting area*

The area under pastures would reflect a balanced approach to farming, the preservation of common land, and grazing ground for livestock. Extremely low ranks obtained by the agriculturally advanced States of Punjab and Haryana indicate the dominance of cultivation and perhaps, stall-feeding.

4. *Percentage area under tree crops to total reporting area*

The area under tree crops would supplement the actual area under forests providing the same benefits of soil/slope stabilization and moisture retention. Again, the States of Punjab and Haryana rank low, while Orissa, Assam and Karnataka score high.

5. *Percentage culturable waste to total reporting area*

The extent of culturable waste would indicate the level of effort expended to utilize available land resources. The greater the area classed under culturable waste, the lower the attempts at utilisation. As borne out by the above explanation, the agriculturally developed States of Punjab and Haryana score highest recording the least percentage area under culturable waste, while Gujarat and Rajasthan score lowest, perhaps attributable to scarcity of water in these States.

6. *Percentage current fallow to NSA*

The proportion of net sown area currently left under fallow reflects the chances of natural rejuvenation of the soil without the fallouts of excessive chemical fertilizer use. Scores again show Punjab ranking lowest which is a fair reflection of the currently falling growth in crop productivity in the State. The two southern States of Andhra Pradesh and Tamil Nadu and the eastern States of Assam and Bihar all have over 25 per cent of their net sown area under current fallow.

7. *Percentage area under foodgrains to Gross Cropped Area*
8. *Cropping intensity*
9. *Yield of foodgrains*

The yield of foodgrains is an accurate indicator not only of agricultural technology, but also environmental conditions – quality of soil, availability of rainfall/irrigation and stability of climatic conditions. Low yield would reflect years of drought/flood and other natural calamities too. Predictably the 'food basket' States of Punjab, Haryana and Tamil Nadu record the highest yields, with the food deficit State of Kerala scoring a surprising fourth place.

10. *Per capita availability of foodgrain*
11. *Percentage of workers in Mining and Quarrying*

The proportion of workers in mining and quarrying to the total workers in the State is indicative of the extent of its extractive activity. This in turn reflects change in landscape, depletion of exhaustible resources and, perhaps, an increase in the incidence of landslips and polluting mine waste.

Constructing the Composite Index

Each of the fifteen selected States was ranked on a scale of one to fifteen with reference to each of the eleven indicators in Set I: QOE. The ranks were assigned in either ascending or descending order depending on the variable in question (i.e. whether it is a positive or negative indicator). Once the ranks for each State were assigned, the ranks were totalled across variables for each State. The composite rank score was then arranged in ascending order with the lowest composite score being assigned rank I, the highest, rank XV. Thus the end result of the exercise is the rank of each State on the quality of life index and the rank of each State on the quality of environment index (Table 3.3).

If we combine these two dimensions in order to derive a single system of ranking based on both QOL and QOE (Tables 3.4 and 3.5), Punjab and Haryana emerge as the top ranking States whereas States like Bihar and Madhya Pradesh are found at the bottom of the scale based on the data for 1991. The sharp change in the

TABLE 3.3: **Composite Indices and Scores: 1991**

Rank	State	Composite Index (Development)	Rank	Composite Index (Environment)
8	Andhra Pradesh	83	12	99
12	Assam	125	6	83.5
15	Bihar	137	10.5*	93.5
5	Gujarat	54	15	118.5
7	Haryana	71	1	61.5
6	Karnataka	70	8	90
3	Kerala	49	13	107
11	Madhya Pradesh	124	10.5*	93.5
2	Maharashtra	41	14	110.5
14	Orissa	131	5	80.5
1	Punjab	40	2	62
10	Rajasthan	117	9*	91
4	Tamil Nadu	53	7	86
13	Uttar Pradesh	128	3	62.5
9	West Bengal	97	4	69

position of various States between 1951 and 1991 may be analysed through a comparison of Tables 3.4 and 3.5. In the early fifties, Kerala and Bombay ranked first and second, respectively, with Rajasthan and Orissa occupying the lowest positions. Significant enhancement in the rank is that of Punjab which stood fourth from the bottom in 1951. Madras retains its third position.

To assess the current status of each State with reference separately to quality of life and quality of environment, the graphical technique introduced in chapter 2 was utilised (Fig.3.1). The graph is divided into nine sectors based on a combination of high, medium and low scores on each of the two dimensions. Fig. 3.1 shows Punjab emerging distinctly with high scores on both dimensions—implying both a high quality of life and a high quality of environment with reference to the other States. Maharashtra and Kerala record a high level of quality of life, but score extremely low on environmental indicators.

TABLE 3.4 **Inter-State Comparison of Index of Sustainable Development (1991)**

State	Index of Sustainable Development	Ranks
Punjab	102	1
Haryana	132.5	2
Tamil Nadu	139	3
Maharashtra	151.5	4
Kerala	156	5
Karnataka	160	6
West Bengal	166	7
Gujarat	172.5	8
Andhra Pradesh	182	9
Uttar Pradesh	190.5	10
Rajasthan	208	11
Assam	208.5	12
Orissa	211.5	13
Madhya Pradesh	217.5	14
Bihar	230.5	15

TABLE 3.5: **Inter-State Comparison of Index of Sustainable Development (1951)**

State	Index of Sustainable Development	Ranks
Kerala	77	1
Bombay	98	2
Madras	100	3
West Bengal	108	4
Mysore	111	5
Bihar	112	6
Uttar Pradesh	115	7
Andhra Pradesh	119	8

(Contd.)

TABLE 3.5: *(Contd.)*

State	Index of Sustainable Development	Ranks
Madhya Pradesh	127	9
Punjab	129	10
Assam	133	11
Orissa	144	12
Rajasthan	153.6	13

Karnataka alone scores medium rank on both indicators. While UP scores high on the environmental scale, it ranks poorly on the quality of life index. The States of Madhya Pradesh and Bihar emerge with low scores on both dimensions of measurement. However, large States such as Uttar Pradesh, Madhya Pradesh, Maharashtra, etc. with their regional diversity and extent may record distorted scores as a result of extreme values in certain spatial units of the States.

The locations of the States with reference to their scores on the two indices also have implications in terms of planning policy. For instance, it is quite evident that while Gujarat, Maharashtra and Kerala need to focus on environmental regeneration, Uttar Pradesh, Orissa, Assam and Rajasthan must stress on improving their quality of life. Table 3.6 sets out strategic implications for each State.

Ranking of States on QOL and QOE – A Comparison of 1950's and 1991

In this section, an attempt is made to compare the relative position of each State with regard to its Quality of Life and Quality of Environment scores both currently (1991) and during the period (1951-58) i.e. in the first decade after and independence.

As data collection and collation for this period poses several problems, not the least of which is the fact that the re-organisation of States took place only after 1956-57, the unit of observation i.e. the States may not be strictly comparable. However, as regards, the relative position of the States. it is simple to identify the modern

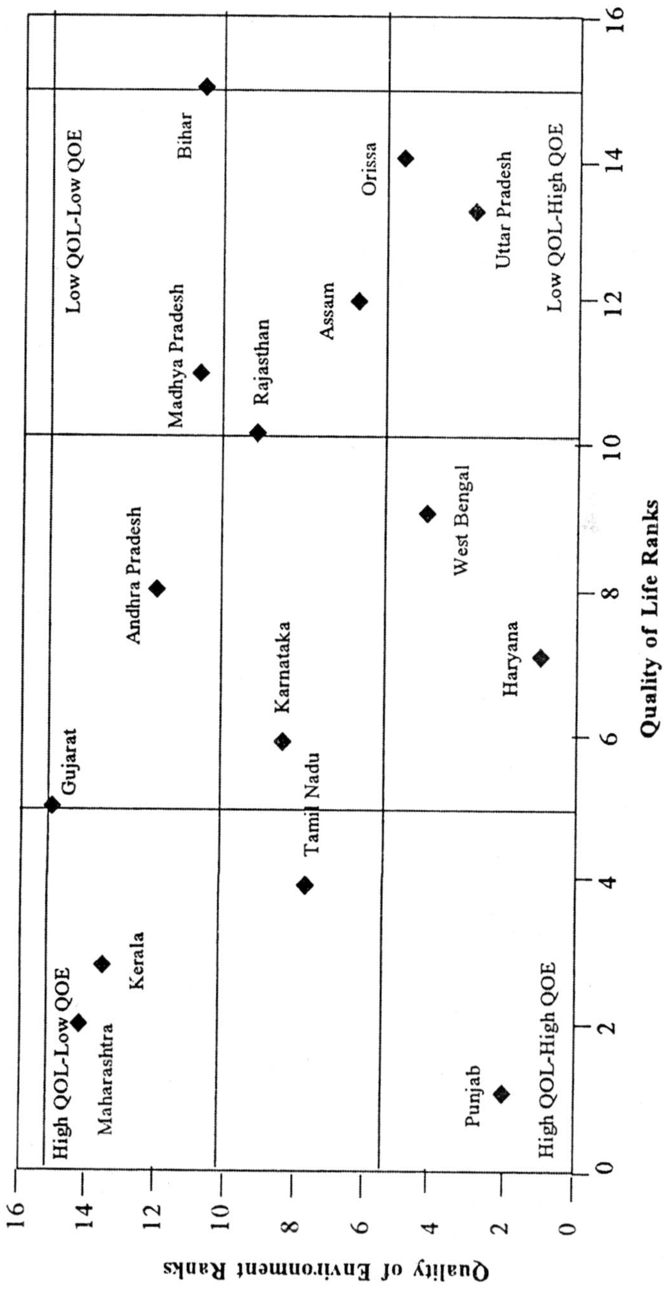

Fig. 3.1: Indian States: Quality of Life *Vs.* Quality of Environment (1991)

TABLE 3.6: **Classification of States by Combination of QOL and QOE Scores**

Type	States	Suggested Strategy
High QOL-High QOE	Punjab	Continue existing development/ environment policies
High QOL-Medium QOE	Tamil Nadu	Stress on environmental rehabilitation
High QOL-Low QOE	Kerala, Maharashtra	Total focus on environmental improvement
Medium QOL-High QOE	Haryana, West Bengal	Focus on environment improving strategies
Medium QOL-Med QOE	Karnataka	Equal emphasis on quality of life and quality of environment
Medium QOL-Low QOE	Andhra Pradesh, Gujarat	Immediate focus on environmental issues. Quality of life needs improvement, but is not the priority
Low QOL-High QOE	Uttar Pradesh	Development and quality of life take priority
Low QOL-Medium QOE	Orissa, Assam, Rajasthan	Immediate priority to development issues
Low QOL- Low QOE	Madhya Pradesh, Bihar	Immediate priority to both development and environment

State units as part or whole of the old (1951) States.

All twenty-two indicators analysed for the year 1991 were not available for the period 1951-58. However, as many as possible were collected. In all, seven indicators of quality of life and ten indicators of environmental quality were analysed. (See Tables 3.7 and 3.8) The indicators are listed below:

Quality of Life Indicators

1. Per capita consumption of electricity (kWh) (1958-59)
2. Length of surfaced roads per sq. km (1958)
3. Number of beds per lakh population (1958)
4. Percentage urban to total population (1951)
5. Sex ratio (1958)

TABLE 3.7: Indian States 1951: Quality of Life Indicators

Rank	State	Per capita Consumption of Electricity (kWh) 1958-59	Rank	State	Length of surfaced roads per sq.km. 1958	Rank	State	No. of Beds per lakh pop. 1958	Rank	State	% Urban Pop. 1951
	1			2			3			4	
1	West Bengal	83.60	1	Bombay	14486.50	1	WB	100.72	1	Bombay	28.28
2	Bombay	65.21	2	UP	13725.75	2	Kerala	84.28	2	WB	24.83
3	Mysore	40.99	3	Bihar	13282.25	3	Punjab	74.40	3	Madras	24.41
4	Madras	38.03	4	Madras	9813.50	4	Mysore	62.49	4	Mysore	22.97
5	Kerala	29.84	5	WB	9149.25	5	Rajasthan	58.11	5	Punjab	19.01
6	Punjab	25.34	6	Rajasthan	9134.50	6	Bombay	46.19	6	Rajasthan	18.50
7	Orissa	18.00	7	AP	8099.00	7	AP	42.79	7	AP	17.40
8	Bihar	15.16	8	MP	6968.50	8	Madras	42.76	8	UP	13.64
9	AP	12.33	9	Mysore	6660.50	9	MP	33.71	9	Kerala	13.14
10	UP	12.13	10	Orissa	4723.00	10	UP	29.51	10	MP	12.02
11	MP	9.27	11	Assam	4488.25	11	Orissa	27.75	11	Bihar	6.77
12	Rajasthan	4.56	12	Punjab	4128.75	12	Bihar	16.22	12	Assam	4.31
13	Assam	2.01	13	Kerala	3726.75	13	Assam	0.00	13	Orissa	4.06

(Contd.)

TABLE 3.7: (*Contd.*)

Rank	State	Sex Ratio 1951	Rank	State	Infant Mortality Rate 1958	Rank	State	% Female literates 1951
	5			6			7	
1	Kerala	1027.73	1	Kerala	49.50	1	Kerala	31.48
2	Orissa	1022.11	2	Mysore	70.90	2	WB	12.18
3	Madras	1007.46	3	Bihar	74.00	3	Bombay	11.00
4	Bihar	989.87	4	Assam	77.40	4	Madras	10.07
5	AP	985.66	5	WB	80.40	5	Mysore	9.17
6	MP	966.93	6	AP	85.90	6	Punjab	8.47
7	Mysore	966.36	7	UP	103.00	7	Assam	7.81
8	Bombay	944.46	8	Madras	103.40	8	AP	6.40
9	Rajasthan	920.98	9	Punjab	108.10	9	Orissa	4.52
10	UP	909.91	10	Bombay	112.60	10	Bihar	3.78
11	Assam	879.34	11	MP	146.70	11	UP	3.56
12	WB	864.52	12	Orissa	155.20	12	MP	3.22
13	Punjab	858.48	13	Rajasthan		13	Rajasthan	2.98

(*Contd.*)

TABLE 3.8: **Indian States 1951: Quality of Environment Indicators**

Rank	State	Percentage Area under Forests 1956-57	Rank	State	Percentage Area under Pastures 1956-57	Rank	State	Percentage Area under Tree Crops 1956-57	Rank	State	Percentage Culturable Waste 1956-57
	1			2			3			4	
1	Assam	33.67	1	Mysore	9.74	1	Assam	8.34	1	WB	0.00
2	MP	31.08	2	MP	6.65	2	WB	8.01	2	Assam	0.77
3	Kerala	25.07	3	Bombay	4.98	3	Kerala	5.41	3	Bombay	2.89
4	Orissa	22.91	4	Orissa	4.74	4	UP	3.98	4	Mysore	3.51
5	Bihar	22.60	5	AP	4.59	5	Orissa	2.98	5	Kerala	4.65
6	AP	20.64	6	Rajasthan	4.04	6	Mysore	2.09	6	Bihar	5.13
7	Mysore	14.41	7	Madras	2.89	7	Madras	2.01	7	Punjab	5.78
8	Madras	13.80	8	Kerala	1.29	8	Bombay	1.42	8	Madras	5.99
9	Bombay	12.81	9	Bihar	1.15	9	AP	0.87	9	UP	6.01
10	UP	12.17	10	Punjab	1.11	10	MP	0.86	10	AP	6.74
11	WB	11.58	11	Assam	1.06	11	Rajasthan	0.14	11	Orissa	9.12
12	Rajasthan	4.21	12	UP	0.09	12	Punjab	0.07	12	MP	9.59
13	Punjab	3.06	13	WB	0.00	13	Bihar	0.00	13	Rajasthan	21.44

(Contd.)

TABLE 3.8: *(Contd.)*

Rank	State	Percentage Current Fallow to NSA 1956-57	Rank	State	Percentage Area under Foodgrains to GCA 1956-57	Rank	State	Cropping Intensity 1956-57
	5			6			7	
1	Bihar	21.76	1	Bihar	94.56	1	Punjab	135.45
2	Madras	17.16	2	UP	86.93	2	Bihar	130.30
3	AP	15.69	3	WB	85.13	3	UP	126.20
4	Rajasthan	13.29	4	MP	82.32	4	Kerala	120.75
5	Orissa	12.53	5	Rajasthan	78.92	5	Madras	118.94
6	Assam	9.32	6	Assam	77.69	6	Assam	117.29
7	Mysore	8.94	7	Orissa	76.46	7	WB	116.78
8	MP	5.33	8	Punjab	74.06	8	MP	113.61
9	Bombay	5.24	9	AP	71.59	9	Rajasthan	110.35
10	Punjab	4.23	10	Madras	69.54	10	AP	109.41
11	Kerala	3.44	11	Mysore	67.50	11	Orissa	107.97
12	UP	3.43	12	Bombay	60.48	12	Bombay	104.66
13	WB		13	Kerala	37.63	13	Mysore	103.22

(Contd.)

TABLE 3.8: *(Contd.)*

Rank	State	Yield of Food-grains (metric Tonnes) 1958-59	Rank	State	Per Capita Avail-ability of Foodgrains (quintals) 1958-59	Rank	State	Percent-age workers in M & Q 1958
	8			9			10	
1	UP	13054.00	1	Bombay	13.40	1	UP	0.00
2	Bombay	9079.00	2	MP	5.03	2	Kerala	0.01
3	MP	9042.00	3	UP	3.83	3	Punjab	0.02
4	Bihar	6574.00	4	Rajasthan	3.49	4	Madras	0.07
5	AP	6297.00	5	Punjab	2.81	5	Assam	0.10
6	Punjab	6177.00	6	AP	1.79	6	Bombay	0.11
7	Rajasthan	5152.00	7	Bihar	1.62	7	AP	0.18
8	Madras	5017.00	8	Mysore	1.29	8	Rajasthan	0.20
9	WB	4595.00	9	WB	0.94	9	MP	0.47
10	Mysore	3564.00	10	Madras	0.81	10	Mysore	0.48
11	Orissa	2393.00	11	Orissa	0.76	11	Orissa	0.66
12	Assam	1719.00	12	Assam	0.34	12	WB	1.03
13	Kerala	925.00	13	Kerala	0.06	13	Bihar	1.28

6. Infant mortality rate (1958)
7. Percentage female literates (1951)

Quality of Environment Indicators

1. Percentage area under forests (1956-57)
2. Percentage area under pastures (1956-57)
3. Percentage area under tree crops (1956-57)
4. Percentage culturable waste (1956-57)
5. Percentage current fallow to Net Sown Area (1956-57)
6. Percentage area under foodgrain to Gross Cropped Area (1956-57)
7. Cropping intensity (1956-57)
8. Yield of foodgrains (metric tonnes per ha. —1958-59)
9. Percentage of workers in Mining and Quarrying (1958)

As can be seen from the above lists, while four indicators of quality of life—(1) Per capita net State domestic product, (2) Percentage of electrified villages, (3) Life expectancy at birth, and (4) Percentage rural households getting two square meals a day which were part of the composite index in 1991 were not available for the fifties, there are also minor variations in some of the indicators which were available, e.g., in place of percent rural infant mortality, the indicator available for 1958 is the general infant mortality rate.

With reference to the quality of environment indicators too, while ten of the eleven indicators analysed for 1991 were available for the decade 1951-61, there is a variation in the first indicator, i.e. instead of percent growth in forest area, the percentage of area under forests to total area has been substituted.

Following the same methodology adopted as in the case of data pertaining to 1991 variables, a composite index of Quality of Life and one of Quality of Environment was computed, (Table 3.9) the ranks obtained by each State on the two sets of scores being used to plot the position of the States. In the case of the 1950s' indicators, there were only thirteen States, so the ranks range from one to thirteen. A comparison of the two graphs Figs 3.1 and 3.2 brings out the change in position of each State over the forty-year period since independence and also indicates the development path being followed by each State over the same period.

TABLE 3.9: **Indian States—Composite Indices and Scores: 1951**

Rank	State	Quality of Life: Score	Rank	Quality of Environment: Score
6	Andhra Pradesh	49	7	70
12	Assam	71	4	62
7	Bihar	51	3	61
4	Bombay	33	5	65
3	Kerala	32	8.5	75
11	Madhya Pradesh	67	2	60
2	Madras	31	6	69
5	Mysore	34	9	77
10	Orissa	64	12.5	80
8	Punjab	54	8.5	75
13	Rajasthan	74.6	11	79
9	Uttar Pradesh	58	1	57
1	West Bengal	28	12.5	80

As can be seen from the graphs, the most dramatic change can be seen in Punjab, which, during the fifties, scored medium ranks with reference to both quality of life and quality of environment. In fact, Fig. 3.2 shows Punjab as a borderline State just escaping low scores on both dimensions. Fig 3.1 shows Punjab as the top ranking State with reference to both sets of indicators and in fact, far outpacing its nearest competitors i.e. Haryana and Tamil Nadu. It must, however, be remembered that the erstwhile State of Punjab included both Haryana and Himachal Pradesh.

The relative position of West Bengal has recorded tremendous improvement in environmental quality, but has deteriorated with reference to quality of life.

The erstwhile presidency of Bombay and the State of Kerala show significant improvement in ranking on the quality of life index, but gain is coupled with a deteriorating environmental status. Tamil Nadu and Uttar Pradesh are the two States recording no change in relative position—neither on quality of life nor on the quality of environment index. Bihar is the only State, which has fallen in rank on both dimensions of development from medium

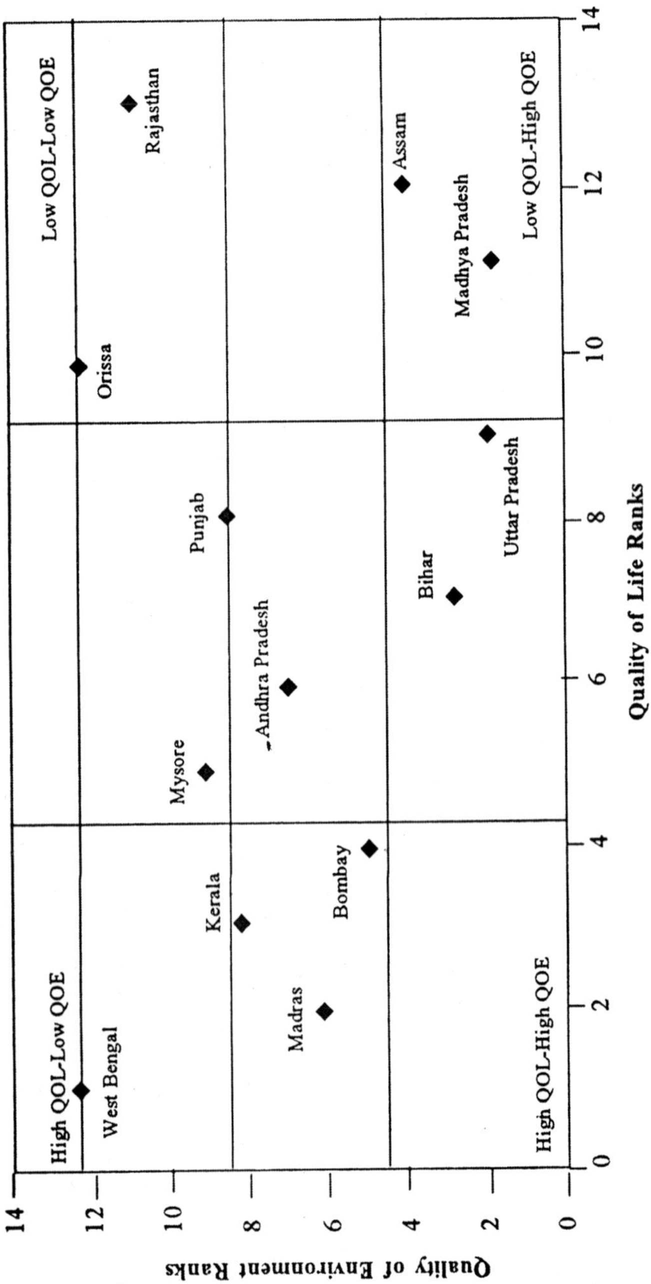

Fig. 3.2: Indian States: Quality of Life *Vs.* Quality of Environment (1951)

QOL – high QOE to low on both facets.

The States of Orissa and Rajasthan record static ranks with reference to quality of life, but have registered an improvement in environmental status. Madhya Pradesh and Assam record a sharply deteriorating environment, while quality of life remains more or less the same.

Table 3.10 details the position of each State in the fifties and the type of development strategy which has been followed.

TABLE 3.10: **Change in Development Strategy: 1951-91**

Type	States	Changes Between 1951-1991 based on development strategy
High QOL – High QOE	—	
High QOL – Med. QOE	Bombay, Madras, Kerala	Bombay, Kerala – Focus on development, environment ignored, Madras (Tamil Nadu) remains static
High QOL – Low QOE	West Bengal	Focus on environment
Med. QOL-High QOE	Bihar, UP	U.P. —no change Bihar —both development and environment scores have fallen
Med QOL-Med. QOE	Andhra Pradesh, Punjab	Punjab—High priority and equal emphasis on the environment and development Andhra Pradesh – quality of life remains static, environment has deteriorated
Med. QOL – Low QOE	Mysore	Mysore – environment has improved, quality of life-static
Low QOL – High QOE	Assam, Madhya Pradesh	Assam – focus on development, environment has deteriorated MP —Quality of life remains same, environment has deteriorated
Low QOL – Med QOE	—	
Low QOL – Low QOE	Orissa, Rajasthan	Orissa, Rajasthan – quality of life remains same, quality of environment, considerable in the case of Orissa, slight in the case of Rajasthan

4

ASSESSING THE SUSTAINABILITY OF A NATURAL REGION

A Natural region can be defined as a homogeneous spatial unit with distinct physical characteristics expressed in the form of topography, climate, soil, natural vegetation and ultimately in the livelihood of the people. The physical homogeneity of the natural region transcends the super-imposed political boundaries. However, locational attributes in terms of accessibility and human inputs in terms of infrastructural development and political will often result in diverse development patterns with differing impacts on the environment.

The case selected for analysis here is the Indian Hindu Kush Himalayan region which forms the north-western and central portions of the Himalayan belt running across the Northern boundary of India. The region with its unique natural characteristics is also typified by a more or less common development pattern – a largely subsistence economy heavily dependent on the natural resource base. As an intrinsic part of the fragile mountain environment zone where the least imbalance in developmental focus can have far reaching repercussions impacting on places as distant as the plains of North India, the assessment of the sustainability of development in the region becomes crucial for policy makers and planners. An attempt is made in this chapter to assess the level of sustainability in the constituent units of the region and to arrive at guidelines for development on the basis of the analysis. As policy formulation and implementation is necessarily within the political framework, the analysis is based on district-wise comparisons.

The Study Area

The Indian Hindu Kush Himalayas form a distinct natural region comprising the States of Jammu and Kashmir with an area of about 2,22,000 sq. km. and Himachal Pradesh about 56,000 sq. km. together with the adjoining hill districts of Uttar Pradesh (51,000 sq. kms.). This great chain of mountain ranges with complex topography is endowed with abundant natural resources including perennial snow-fed streams, innumerable species of flora and fauna and a rich cultural heritage. Low population densities, little urbanisation and low literacy rates characterise the region. For a mountain region, the proportion of forest area is abysmally low, except for the hills of Uttar Pradesh which still have about a third of their area under dense forest cover.

Development in the region is characterised by unsustainable resource use, increasing population coupled with out-migration, significant reduction in forest cover, increased frequency of floods and land-slides, greater incidence of poverty and an introverted subsistence economy largely dependent on extractive primary activities. This economic system in turn has imposed on the mountain inhabitants the burden of perpetual poverty. Since poverty and environmental degradation reinforce each other (WCED 1987), the challenge posed to the development planner is not merely eradication of poverty within the limiting environmental conditions, but the achievement of sustainable development with reasonable living standards for the inhabitants of the mountain eco-system.

The region consists of 34 districts, 14 in the State of Jammu and Kashmir, 12 in Himachal Pradesh and 8 in Uttar Pradesh (Table 4.1).

Data Base and Selection of Indicators

Data on selected development and environmental indicators was collated for all thirty-four districts (see Table 4.2). The data pertains to the year 1981 as this is the only time period during which comparable data for all three States was available. The selected development indicators were seven in number relating to demographic characteristics and social amenities. They are listed below:

1. Population density (persons per sq. km.)
2. Percentage of female literates to total female population
3. Percentage of workers to total population
4. Percentage of agricultural labour to total workers
5. Percentage of electrified villages to total villages
6. Percentage of villages with drinking water to total villages
7. Beds in allopathic hospitals/dispensaries per hundred thousand population

TABLE 4.1: **Administrative Units of the Indian Hindu Kush Himalayan Region**

Jammu & Kashmir	Himachal Pradesh	Uttar Pradesh
1. Anantnag	15. Bilaspur	27. Uttarkashi
2. Badgam	16. Hamirpur	28. Chamoli
3. Baramulla	17. Kangra	29. Pauri Garhwal
4. Doda	18. Kinnaur	30. Tehri Garhwal
5. Jammu	19. Chamba	31. Garhwal
6. Kargil	20. Kullu	32. Pithoragarh
7. Kathua	21. Lahaul & Spiti	33. Almora
8. Kupwara	22. Mandi	34. Nainital
9. Leh	23. Shimla	
10. Pulwama	24. Sirmaur	
11. Poonch	25. Solan	
12. Rajouri	26. Una	
13. Srinagar		
14. Udhampur		

Among the demographic indicators, population density and female literacy have been considered as positive indicators of development. In the hill region, the very low population densities result in thresholds too low to support even the minimum required infrastructure. Thus, contrary to the general situation in the country where high population densities imply negative impacts on the environment, the reverse holds true for the hills. The level of

TABLE 4.2: **Quality of Life and Life of Environment Indicators for Districts**

Variables District	Pop. Density (per sq.km.)	Rank	% Female Literacy	Rank	% Workers to Total Pop.	Rank	% Agri-cultural Labour to Total Workers	Rank	% of Elec. Villages to Total Villages	Rank
	1		2		3		4		5	
Uttarkashi	23.82	30	9.17	30	52.12	3	0.57	3	34.52	27
Chamoli	39.93	28	18.34	19.5	44.74	7	0.33	2	23.86	31
Tehri	112.58	21	18.34	19.5	44.69	8	0.28	1	15.99	34
Dehradun	246.65	6	9.42	28	32.56	18	7.94	33	42.76	26
Garhwal	117.26	19	42.03	2	36.21	13	0.82	7	18.88	32
Pithoragarh	55.25	25	27.13	11	38.33	11	0.65	5	17.77	33
Almora	140.64	15	20.3	15	31.51	23	1.57	11	27.74	29
Nainital	167.28	10	20.27	16	31.68	20.5	19.09	34	54.94	21
Chamba	47.66	26	24.11	13	35.12	14	0.63	4	54.16	22
Kangra	172.64	9	13.59	23	26.67	31	5.15	26	64.92	16
Hamirpur	284.21	4	39.93	4	24.72	33	2.11	14	61.52	19
Una	206.12	8	45.17	1	23.49	34	6.33	30	65.17	15
Bilaspur	211.97	7	40.62	3	31.8	19	1.41	10	73.11	11
Mandi	163.25	12	34.76	5	37.43	12	0.87	8	52.85	24
Kullu	43.38	27	27.45	10	45.09	6	1.74	12	55.03	20

(*Contd.*)

TABLE 4.2: *(Contd.)*

	1		2		3		4		5	
Lahaul & Spiti	2.32	33	18.96	18	59.09	1	2.37	16.5	42.99	25
Shimla	99.58	24	15.44	21	46.41	4	2.96	22	66.41	14
Solan	156.65	13	29.48	8	34.52	15	2.37	16.5	53.17	23
Sirmaur	108.66	22	28.9	9	40.22	10	2.13	15	77.1	10
Kinnaur	9.3	31	19.79	17	54.67	2	5.31	27	68.83	13
Anantnag	164.75	11	31.46	7	31.68	20.5	2.8	21	99.36	2
Badgam	267.88	5	10.94	26	32.81	17	2.66	19	100	1
Baramulla	146.06	14	8.02	31	31.43	24	3.86	24	93.32	5
Doda	36.38	29	9.57	27	33.48	16	2.65	18	61.96	18
Jammu	304.62	2	7.34	32	26.66	32	5.46	28	88.62	7
Kargil	4.7	32	32.24	6	45.33	5	3.25	23	25.2	30
Kathua	139.24	16	3.14	34	28.82	28	5.67	29	90.11	6
Kupwara	138.19	17	21.25	14	30.37	25	6.88	31	84.21	8
Leh	0.83	34	4.88	33	43.55	9	7.36	32	30.56	24
Pulwama	289.04	3	12.09	24	29.04	27	2.05	13	98.52	4
Punch	133.93	18	9.21	29	27.72	29	4.04	25	80.38	9
Rajouri	115.02	20	11.24	25	27.59	30	1.29	9	64.4	17
Srinagar	317.92	1	14.32	22	30.12	26	2.68	20	99	3
Udhampur	99.7	23	24.66	12	31.62	22	0.78	6	73.1	12

(Contd.)

TABLE 4.2: *(Contd.)*

Variables Districts	% Villages with Drinking Water	Rank	Beds in Allo. Hosp./ Disp. per lakh Pop. (Nos.)	Rank	% Area under Forest	Rank	% Barren Area	Rank	% Area under Cult Waste	Rank
	6		7		8		9		10	
Uttarkashi	54.91	10	44	12	88.61	2	0.77	7	3.03	19
Chamoli	51.88	12	30	14	57.75	7	19.44	33	2.27	22
Tehri	27.78	26	12	21	89.84	1	1.81	12	14.65	2
Dehradun	65.58	7	27	15	73.21	5	0.61	6	3.87	16
Garhwal	25.65	27	19	17	83.75	3	4.66	23	6.41	10
Pithoragarh	73.02	5	25	16	37.3	12	3.32	22	6.72	7
Almora	28.27	25	14	19	73.25	4	6.54	28	12.84	3
Nainital	77.98	4	13	20	59.25	6	0.92	9	4.51	13
Chamba	51.69	13	154	4	38.66	9	0.38	5	0.83	29
Kangra	53.2	11	106	6.5	32.84	13	5.25	24	25.03	1
Hamirpur	40.21	17	55	11	12.55	20	17.7	32	7.67	5
Una	67.5	6	35	13	18.43	17	20.31	34	6.5	9
Bilaspur	38.42	19	104	8	9.83	22	5.38	26	3.65	17
Mandi	35.75	21	96	9	38.04	10	3.16	19	0.94	28
Kullu	81.66	2	87	10	0	32.5	1.14	10	0.6	30

(Contd.)

TABLE 4.2: *(Contd.)*

	6		7		8		9		10	
Lahaul & Spiti	78.72	3	106	6.5	3.15	24	0.06	1	0.19	32
Shimla	60.97	8	218	1	9.53	23	2.33	15	2.48	21
Solan	30.21	24	217	2	10.13	21	5.33	25	6.71	8
Sirmaur	41.02	15	137	5	17.62	17	2.58	16	4.63	12
Kinnaur	96.1	1	166	3	0.01	31	0.35	4	0.52	31
Anantnag	40.8	16	5	29.67	0.12	30	2.16	13	2.13	23
Badgam	33.9	22	7	24	0.51	20	1.19	11	2.49	20
Baramulla	42.8	14	6	26.25	0.28	27	3.3	21	1.62	26
Doda	30.6	23	15	18	18.8	16	2.65	17	1.78	25
Jammu	55.7	9	6	26.25	15.58	19	15.41	31	9.45	4
Kargil	5.8	33	—	—	0	32.5	0.3	2.5	0.34	33
Kathua	39.7	18	11	22	26.3	14	10.88	30	3.29	18
Kupwara	20.3	29	5	29.67	0.17	29	0.89	8	1.96	24
Leh	2.2	34	—	—	—	—	0.3	2.5	0.05	34
Pulwama	36.2	20	5	29.67	0.49	27	2.95	18	3.99	15
Punch	8.5	32	6	26.25	20.49	15	3.27	20	4.76	11
Rajauri	15.2	31	6	26.25	35.18	11	9.98	29	6.94	6
Srinagar	19	30	3	32	0.57	25	2.29	14	1.45	27
Udhampur	25.3	28	9	23	41.52	8	5.68	27	4.39	14

(Contd.)

TABLE 4.2: *(Contd.)*

Variables Districts	Cropping Intensity	Rank	Foodgrain Prod. Per Capita per day (gms.)	Rank	% Area under Pastures	Rank
	11		12		13	
Uttarkashi	158.02	15	754.65	10	2.4752994	22
Chamoli	154.1	19	547.82	17	2.9128767	21
Tehri	163.54	12	584.06	16	3.2990274	19
Dehradun	157.07	16	275.66	19	0.0045337	31
Garhwal	149.11	22	600.43	15	5.7965074	14
Pithoragarh	175.29	6	832.16	5	8.2139792	10
Almora	166.3	9	667.34	12	9.4258124	9
Nainital	168.11	8	1208.59	1	0.1741242	30
Chamba	156.57	17	716.44	11	57.352175	1
Kangra	160.64	13	612.08	13	2.2059592	23
Hamirpur	182.52	4	773.84	8	6.2701252	13
Una	165.34	10	769.4	9	4.9675325	16
Bilaspur	188.9	2	803.34	6	38.090831	3
Mandi	177.39	5	911.29	2	32.25519	4
Kullu	152.07	20	890.6	4	0.0005452	32

(Contd.)

TABLE 4.2: *(Contd.)*

	11		12		13	
Lahaul & Spiti	104.56	30	223.87	20	10.327069	8
Shimla	150.6	21	608.06	14	24.732216	5
Solan	158.29	14	776.71	7	39.381715	2
Sirmaur	184.08	3	909.12	3	22.521062	16
Kinnaur	124.37	26	338.08	18	0.4135291	29
Anantnag	116.38	28	56.35	29	2.1084337	25
Badgam	103.87	31	67.47	25	5.0561634	15
Baramulla	100.96	33	52.26	30	2.8799041	21
Doda	119.7	25	60.38	27	0.6746215	28
Jammu	194.27	1	76.96	24	3.5540846	18
Kargil	111.56	29	5.73	34	—	—
Kathua	169.27	7	77.18	23	4.2395323	17
Kupwara	100.04	34	58.33	28	2.1408155	24
Leh	102	32	6.61	33	—	—
Pulwama	129.27	24	63.7	26	6.4699571	12
Punch	141.92	23	183.56	21	10.804659	7
Rajouri	164.53	11	33.9	31	6.6038023	11
Srinagar	113.59	27	16.38	32	1.3056553	26
Udhampur	156.37	18	84.04	22	2.918022	20

female literacy as a positive indicator of development needs no explanation, as it has proved reflective of health, nutrition, cleanliness, education and other quality of life indicators in all developing countries. What needs to be emphasized in the current context, however, is that in the Himalayan region, particularly the U.P. Himalayas, large scale out-migration of young males in the working age group because of both push and pull factors, have resulted in an economy totally dependent on female labour and entrepreneurship. The importance of female literacy, in this context, cannot be over emphasised.

The other two demographic indicators i.e. percentage of workers to total population and percentage of landless labourers to total workers are both taken as negative. In the barely subsis-tence agricultural economy which exists in most of these hill districts and lack of alternative employment opportunities, a high proportion of workers implies more members of the family being forced to join the work force in order to eke out a pittance to survive. The low proportion of cultivable area attributable to the difficult terrain and steep slopes coupled with generations of traditional agriculture have resulted in highly fragmented and marginal land holdings. In such a situation, the proportion of land-less labour assumes added significance in terms of carrying capacities.

The indicators relating to the level of development in terms of the availability of basic social amenities are all positive. The three selected indicators relate to the availability of electricity (an indicator of all round development), clean drinking water (a basic necessity) and health care (in terms of hospital beds).

The state of the environment is reflected in six environmental indicators listed below:

1. Percentage area under forests
2. Percentage area under pastures
3. Percentage culturable waste
4. Percentage barren and uncultivable land
5. Cropping intensity
6. Per capita production of foodgrains per day

While the proportion of green area under forests and pastures as a positive indicator especially in the mountains needs no explanation, the proportion of culturable wasteland as a positive indicator implies the availability of land for expansion of agricultural/pastoral activities without negative impact on the environment. The proportion of barren and uncultivable land is a negative indicator.

The last two indicators are not strictly environmental, but reflect human utilisation of the given environment. A higher cropping intensity implying proportionately better use of the sown area and the availability of foodgrain per capita reflecting the sustainability of the district in terms of providing food locally for its own population.

Each of the thirty-four districts has been ranked on the thirteen indicators positively or negatively as explained above. Based on the composite index of all the thirteen indicators it is possible to rank each of the 34 districts (Table 4.3). Broadly speaking, districts of Himachal Pradesh rank highest followed by districts in Uttar Pradesh hills and Jammu and Kashmir. However, remote and inaccessible mountain districts of Himachal such as Lahaul and Spiti and Kinnaur and Chamoli in Uttar Pradesh do rank much lower on the scale than other districts of these States. A composite index has been computed separately for the development indicators and for the environment indicators by adding the ranks scored against each indicator by each district and a scatter graph has been plotted (Fig. 4.1).

TABLE 4.3: **Composite Index of Ranks obtained on Development and Environment Scores**

Districts	Composite Index of Development	Composite Index of Environment
1	2	3
Uttarkashi	144	75
Chamoli	134	119
Tehri	149	62
Dehradun	132	93
Garhwal	126	87
Pithoragarh	119	62

(Contd.)

TABLE 4.3: *(Contd.)*

1	2	3
Almora	126	65
Nainital	119	67
Chamba	103	72
Kangra	92	87
Hamirpur	71	82
Una	74	95
Bilaspur	74	50
Mandi	102	68
Kullu	110	128
Lahaul & Spiti	136	115
Shimla	121	99
Solan	106	79
Sirmaur	101	58
Kinnaur	125	139
Anantnag	101	148
Badgam	115	128
Baramulla	125	159
Doda	152	138
Jammu	107	97
Kargil	154	131
Kathua	132	109
Kupwara	134	147
Leh	187	101
Pulwama	168	122
Punch	145	97
Rajouri	133	99
Srinagar	117	151
Udhampur	117	109

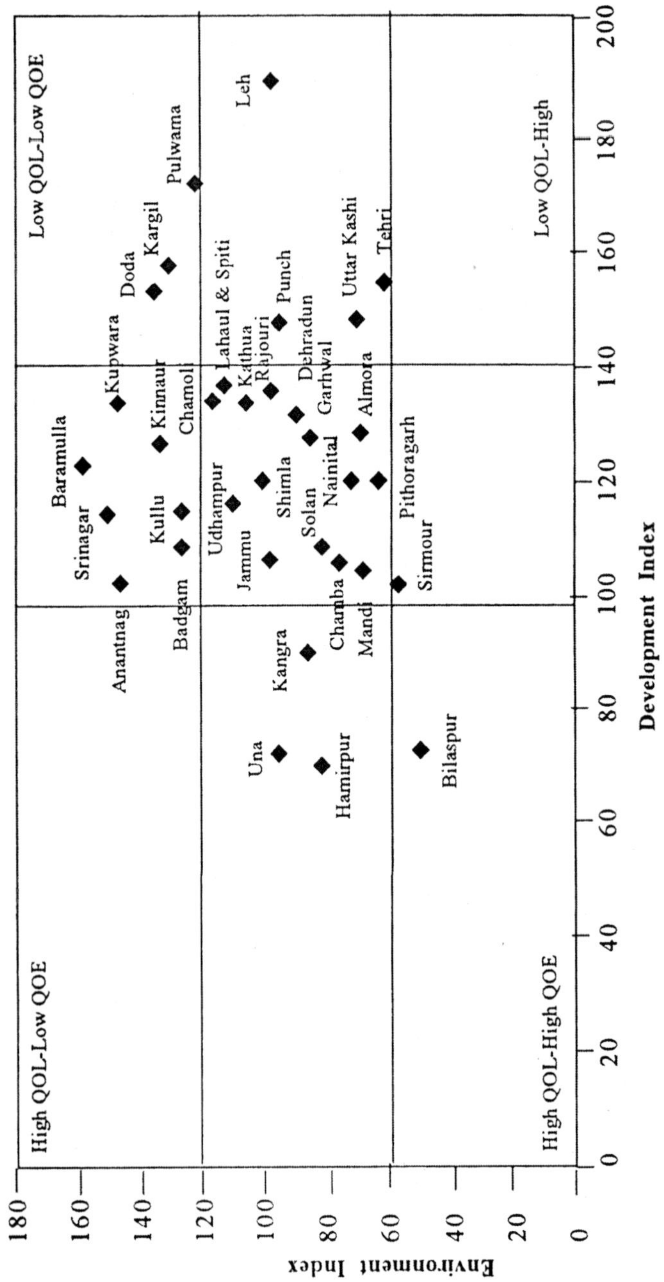

Fig. 4.1: Hindu Kush Himalayan Region: Levels of Environment and Development

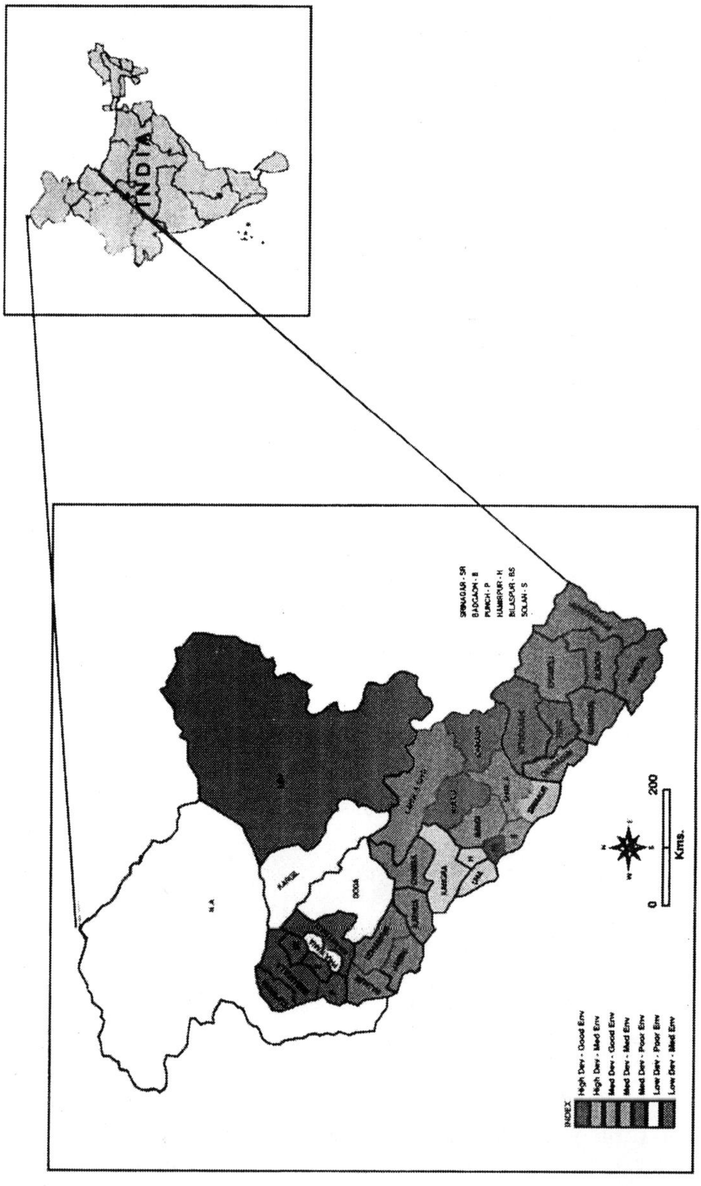

Fig. 4.2 : Hindu Kush Himalayan Region : Relative Levels of Quality of Life and Environment - Spatial Distribution

Environment and Development—A Classification of Districts

As can be seen from the scatter graph, the districts seem to naturally fall into seven groups ranging from low-low (low development - low environment) on the upper right hand corner of the graph to high-high (high development - high environment) on the lower left hand corner of the graph. To facilitate the identification of the position of each district on the graph, all the districts have been individually labelled.

The spatial distribution of districts in the different development-environment categories can be seen in Fig. 4.2. Poor environmental scores are concentrated in the extreme western portion of the region in the districts of Kupwara, Baramulla, Srinagar, Anantnag, Badgam, Doda, Kargil and Pulwama as well as the two central pockets of Kullu and Kinnaur. Districts scoring low on the development scale are again concentrated in the west consisting of Leh, Kargil, Doda, Pulwama and Punch. On both developmental and environmental scales, the western portion of the region scores low as compared to the rest. Bilaspur stands out as the only district scoring high on both development and environment fronts.

Table 4.4 classifies the districts according to the development and environmental scores obtained by them and suggested strategies for development. Broadly stated, strategies giving priority to environmental regeneration have been suggested for the greater part of Jammu & Kashmir and certain pockets of Himachal Pradesh (Kullu and Kinnaur). Development strategies need immediate attention in Uttarkashi and Tehri districts of UP and the Ladakh and Kashmir sub-divisions of Jammu & Kashmir.

Index of Sustainable Development

A composite index of sustainable development applied to the Hindu Kush Himalayan Region (Table 4.5) reveals very broadly that the districts of Himachal Pradesh rank highest in terms of sustainable development followed by the Uttar Pradesh hill districts. Lowest on the scale are the districts of Jammu and Kashmir. However, the more remote and inaccessible mountain districts of Himachal Pradesh such as Lahaul and Spiti and Kinnaur and Chamoli in Uttar Pradesh do rank much lower on the

TABLE 4.4: **Relative Levels of Development and Environment—Classification of Districts**

Type	Districts	Suggested Strategy
High-Development - Good Environment	Bilaspur (HP)	Continue existing development / environment policies
High Development - Medium Environment	Kangra, Hamirpur, Una (HP)	Stress on environmental rehabilitation
Medium Development - Good Environment	Sirmour (HP)	Emphasis on development
Medium Development - Medium Environment	Rajouri, Udhampur, Jammu, Kathua (J&K) Chamba, Lahaul & Spiti, Mandi, Solan, Shimla (HP) Dehradun, Garhwal, Chamoli, Almora, Nainital, Pithoragarh (UP)	Equal emphasis on development and environment
Medium Development - Poor Environment	Kupwara, Baramulla, Srinagar, Anantnag, Badgam (J&K) Kullu, Kinnaur (HP)	Immediate stress on environmental regeneration, development important, but secondary
Low Development - Poor Environment	Kargil, Doda, Pulwama (J&K)	Immediate priority to both environment and development
Low Development - Medium Environment	Leh, Punch (J&K) Uttarkashi, Tehri (UP)	Immediate emphasis on development, environment also needs attention

scale than the other districts of these States.

Taken in consonance with the policy guidelines indicated in Table 4.3, this table can help prioritise the allocation of development interventions and financial assistance.

TABLE 4.5: **Index of Sustainability (Districts of Hindu Kush Himalayas – 1981)**

Districts	Index of Sustainable Development	Ranks
Bilaspur	124	1
Hamirpur	153	2
Sirmour	159	3
Una	169	4
Mandi	170	5
Chamba	175	6
Kangra	179	7
Pithoragarh	181	8
Solan	185	9
Nainital	186	10
Almora	191	11
Jammu	204	12
Tehri	211	13
Garhwal	213	14
Uttar Kashi	219	15
Shimla	220	16
Dehradun	225	17
Udhampur	226	18
Rajouri	232	19
Kullu	238	20
Kathua	241	21
Punch	242	22
Badgam	243	23
Anantnag	249	24
Lahaul & Spiti	251	25
Chamoli	253	26
Kinnaur	264	27
Srinagar	268	28
Kupwara	281	29
Baramulla	284	30
Kargil	285	31
Leh	288	32
Doda	290	33
Pulwama	290	34

5

ASSESSING AND PLANNING FOR SUSTAINABILITY AT MICRO-LEVEL

The search for a common indicator or a set of indicators, which can be used to monitor sustainability at all levels from the national or country level to the micro or village/town level has led us through the previous four chapters, wherein various sets of indicators and diverse methods, both quantitative and graphical, were developed. As far as possible, the choice of indicators was limited to roughly similar variables, which are easily available either directly, or through simple computations.

While the indicators and methods used so far—at country, regional and district levels—were based on secondary data and scaling, assessing sustainability at micro-level calls for a different approach. For one, data at micro-level has to be generated either through field surveys or through estimations and projections. Secondly, at this level, macro concepts may not be relevant. Assessing the sustainability of a town or a village or group of villages must necessarily involve the people who live there and interact with the environment. Both the opportunities and the hazards or threats posed by the environmental setting become part of the local life style and development pattern. It is only if development plans are in consonance with the environment together with the full awareness and involvement of the community that long-term sustainability becomes achievable. Thus developing indicators through participatory techniques becomes essential.

This chapter is divided into two sections, the first focussing on a rural area – the Himalayan Mountain Villages of Chakrata Block – a remote, fairly inaccessible and poorly developed region, the second on a rapidly growing, extremely accessible mountain resort town – Mussoorie. Each of the selected areas has its own advantages and its own problems. Both areas are located in the 'environmentally fragile' designated zone of the Himalayas where the balance between environment and development is extremely delicate and can easily be tipped either way by thoughtless development plans or planning which is unacceptable to the people.

Both the case studies presented here are part of larger research projects conducted by the National Society for Promotion of Development Administration, Research and Training (NSDART) Mussoorie.

THE CASE OF MOUNTAIN VILLAGES IN CHAKRATA BLOCK, DEHRADUN DISTRICT, UTTAR PRADESH

That the sustainability of development projects and programmes is in a large measure due to the participation of the target group needs no reiteration. The success ratio of projects where the local populace have been involved has been widely documented and publicised with the result that government and non-government agencies have come to accept people's participation as a major component in project/programme formulation, implementation and monitoring. However, more often involving the people has been largely limited to the implementation stage. The built-in mind set of the planner/administrator formulating the ideal plan, communicating it to the people and involving them in its implementation with a view to long-term sustainability, still persists. This, perhaps, accounts for the petering out of many ambitious projects even when the target group was involved in their implementation. The practice of imposing a plan from above, although based on detailed survey and data analysis often results in imposing unwanted projects on the local people, when their priorities may lie in a different direction. This is particularly so in the case of urban based planners whose perceptions of the problems in an altogether alien rural environment may be less than realistic. The problem becomes even more complex when gender differences are taken into consideration.

While the above observations are based on the experiences garnered in the process of project evaluation, it was felt that a more detailed analysis of people's participation in the formulation of development plans was warranted. Whether the discrepancy between people's and planners' observations priorities is sufficiently large to justify a modification of the plan, whether certain problem areas are so overwhelming that they override both cultural, area specific and gender differences can only be answered through a detailed analysis.

This chapter attempts to analyse the perceptions of the local people and the planner in a remote mountain region of the Garhwal Himalayas. In January 1996, a village level survey of the Chakrata Block, Dehradun district was carried out with the objective of preparing a Five-Year Plan.

The Study Area

Chakrata block located in the N.W. corner of the State of Uttar Pradesh forms the northernmost block of the Dehradun district (Fig. 5.1). This Himalayan region comprises rugged and mountainous, densely forested terrain enclosed between two main ridges-one separating the watersheds of the Tons and the Yamuna, the other separating the watersheds of the Tons and Shallongad and extending on the various spurs descending from them. Elevation ranges between 400 m to over 3000 m with steep and precipitous slopes.

Chakrata with a total of 154 inhabited villages is the most poorly developed block of the district. The greater part of the population (65 per cent) belongs to the Scheduled Tribes, while as much as 28 per cent are classified in the Scheduled Caste category. Employment is largely in the primary sector – cultivation, livestock rearing and horticulture. Literacy levels are dismally low averaging around 16 per cent. The gender bias is evident in the sex ratio and the literacy levels which capture the low socio-economic status of women. As regards infrastructure, only 39 per cent of the villages get regular water supply and barely 28 per cent get regular electric power.

Methodology

During the field study conducted in the area to canvass questionnaires in the traditional manner, a series of PRA exercises were held at six central places in Chakrata, viz. Atal, Eithan, Haja-Dasau, Quansi, Sawada, and Kathiyan.

The method adopted was simple and unstructured. The researcher/planner went and stood in the village market and began explaining the purpose of his visit to a small group of villagers. In a few minutes a fairly large crowd, sometimes as many as fifty people, had gathered and enthusiastically participated in the exercise. Before beginning the exercise, a list of participants, the villages to which they belonged, and their caste/profession was made out. As each of the six villages visited was a central place (market/service centre), the participants came from a number of surrounding villages (see Fig. 5.1 and Appendix 5.1).

The villagers participating represented diverse interest/caste groups including high castes such as brahmans and rajputs, scheduled tribes, and scheduled castes mainly the Koltas (black-smith), Baggis (drummers) and Harijans. Landless agricultural labour, marginal farmers and small cultivators were also represented.

The researcher/planner played the role of the facilitator. The people were informed of the purpose of the gathering and the discussion was initiated by explaining the importance of identifying the problems faced by the village community. The participants were asked to begin by identifying all possible problems faced by them. When the list of problems was ready, they were asked to prioritise them. Separate groups for men and women were made, as women tend to be more vocal when their male folk are not present. Later the researcher made out a list of problems which he identified on the basis of observation and prioritised them.

In all the six PRA exercises conducted in the area, it was found that the villagers were very co-operative and willing to identify problems faced by their own village as well as those faced by the surrounding villages. As a follow-up, the problems identified by the villagers were discussed with block officials at the block headquarters—Chakrata, and also with the village level workers. In most cases, the views expressed by the officials were similar to those expressed by the villagers.

For the purpose of the analysis, only the first six needs/problems prioritised by the villagers were used.

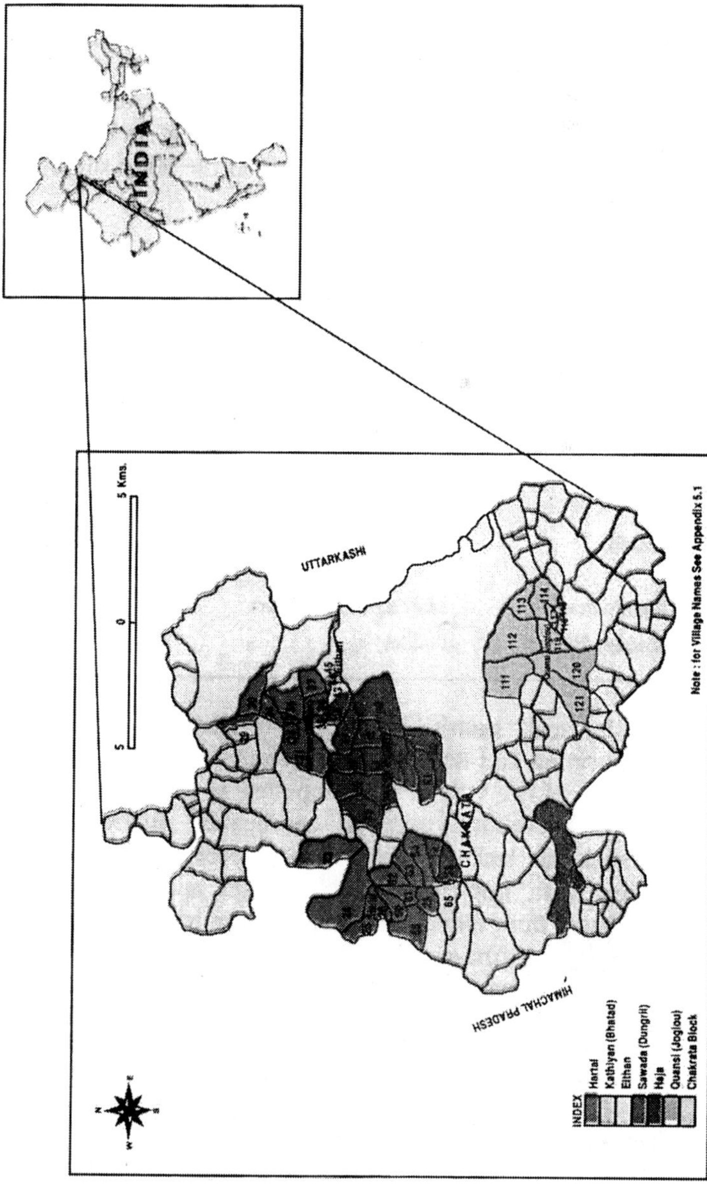

Fig. 5.1 : Chakrata : Location Central Places and Villages Represented in PRA

Village-wise Response

The village of Atal located in the Western corner of Chakrata bordering the neighbouring State of Himachal Pradesh formed the meeting place for fifteen villages, (including Atal) twelve from U.P. and three from H.P. This group of villages is at an elevation of 1000-2000 m which is relatively lower than the other surveyed villages in the block.

TABLE 5.1: **Village Atal: Priority Areas**

Sl. No.	Male	Female	Researcher
1.	Unemployment	Education	Unemployment
2.	Accessibility	Unemployment	Education
3.	Health	Fuel-wood	Teachers absent from schools
4.	Schools	Health	Poor medical facilities
5.	Communication	Marriage-expenditure	
6.	Drinking Water	Fodder	

Unemployment, health and the non-availability of medical facilities, education and inadequate educational facilities were the major priorities of the villagers participating in the exercise. The researcher's observations were in consonance. Infrastructural problems such as lack of .hospital and poor communication network vied with implementation problems such as teachers remaining absent from schools and doctors from health centres.

Analysing the first-six priority areas given by the male participants, female participants and the investigator (Table 5.1), only three common issues emerged i.e. unemployment, health and education. Women's concern with the availability of fodder and fuel did not seem to register with the other participants, Strangely enough, while female literacy is extremely low (less than 5 per cent) in the region, women have rated education as the first priority for planning. This concern with education of the women participants was evident throughout the exercise.

The village of Eithan located in the northern section of the block formed the centre for Eithan itself and two neighbouring villages of Sarani and Patud. These villages lie in a relatively inaccessible area at an elevation of 2000-3000 m above sea level.

TABLE 5.2: **Village Eithan: Priority Areas**

Sl. No.	Male	Female	Researcher
1.	Health	Toilets	Education (literacy)
2.	School (building)	Health	Maternity Care
3.	Horticulture	Education (Literacy)	Awareness
4.	Electricity	Fuel	Poor Infrastructure in schools
5.	Road	Fodder	Marketing
6.	Bank	Roads	

Health and education were the priority areas stressed by all three classes of participants (Table 5.2). While both the women and the researcher felt that in education, illiteracy was the major problem, men tended to emphasise the lack of school buildings. With regard to health, the researcher felt that top priority must be given to maternity care, while the local participants did not specify details. Both men and women felt that the lack of roads was a major problem, which the researcher did not perceive. Female emphasis on fuel and fodder and male emphasis on horticulture and electricity and banking facilities is an obvious reflection of the gender based job sharing system.

Haja-Dasau located in the south-west of the block was the meeting ground for its own villagers and those from the three neighbouring villages of Dasau, Matiyana and Kritrauli located at an altitude of 1500-2000 m above sea level. It is linked by one non-metalled road.

From the responses tabulated in Table 5.3, health emerges as the single common priority of all three classes of participants. Both the villagers and the researcher felt that health problems, particularly the lack of medical facilities was their first priority.

While the villagers perceived education as a priority area, women rating it as second only to health, the researcher did not feel that education was a problem in the area.

The emphasis of women on fuel and fodder throughout the Chakrata block was also evident in this group of villages and following the regular pattern was totally unperceived by the local men or the researcher.

TABLE 5.3: **Village : Haja-Dasau : Priority Areas**

Sl. No.	Male	Female	Researcher
1.	Roads	Health	Health
2.	Health	Education	Lack of agricultural inputs
3.	Unemployment	Lack of cottage industries	Lack of agricultural extension facilities
4.	Schools	Toilets	Marketing
5.	Irrigation	Fuel-wood	Storage
6.	Electricity	Fodder	Roads

Lack of agricultural inputs was stressed by the researcher as well as the male villagers. However, the local men ranked the availability of agricultural inputs, particularly irrigation, way below problems affecting their quality of life such as health and education. The researcher, however, felt that this item deserved a higher rating.

The need for roads was the highest priority of the male villagers and was perceived as an area requiring attention by the researcher as well. Women, however, did not give any importance to roads.

The village of Quansi located in the south central portion of the block formed the central point where participants from nine neighbouring villages met and together with the local villagers took part in the PRA exercise. Located at a height of 2000-3000 m, this block of villages is bordered on the north by a densely forested area. This geographic location significantly affected the responses of the participants, particularly the women.

Of the six group exercises undertaken in the area, this stands out as the only group of women who did not rate fodder and fuel as a problem. Obviously, the adjacent forest area supplies the local requirements.

It may be noted that once the traditional female concerns of fodder and fuelwood collection have been eliminated, there is remarkable consonance between the views of all three sets of participants. At least three common priority areas emerged i.e. health, education and irrigation with similar priority ratings being given by the local men and women and in some cases, by the researcher.

TABLE 5.4: **Village Quansi: Priority Areas**

Sl. No.	Male	Female	Researcher
1.	Health	Health (maternity care)	Health (medical facilities)
2.	Roads	Unemployment	Accessibility
3.	Education	Toilets	Irrigation
4.	Water Supply	Education	Education (infrastructure/ teachers)
5.	Irrigation	Irrigation	
6.	Poor agricultural infrastructure		

The problem of accessibility was, however, not ranked as a priority area by women, although both the male villagers and the researcher ranked it as second most important.

Sawada located in the centre of Chakrata block formed the meeting ground for thirteen villages. Topographically, the area is a mountainous one with villages nestled at a height of 2000-3000 m above sea level.

Once again, female concerns centered on the problems of fodder and fuelwood collection and also the provision of basic amenities like toilets. The only area which was of common concern to all three participating groups was education ranked fourth in the list of priorities by both male villages and the researcher, but only sixth by the local women.

Health, particularly the lack of health care facilities was ranked third in importance by both women and the researcher, while the local men did not seem to perceive the lack of medical facilities.

The low level of literacy and lack of awareness prevailing in the area was emphasised by the researcher. However, the local emphasis was more on the provision of roads, electricity, basic amenities like water supply both for drinking and irrigation, banking facilities, etc.

TABLE 5.5: **Village Sawada: Priority Areas**

Sl. No.	Male	Female	Researcher
1.	Roads	Fodder	Illiteracy
2.	Electricity	Fuel	Awareness
3.	Water supply	Health	Poor health facilities
4.	Education	Toilets	Education (non-availability of teachers)
5.	Bank	Unemployment	
6.	Irrigation	Education	Marketing

The village of Kathiyan located in the north of the block formed the centre for itself and nine surrounding villages. The group of villages was representative of the typical high altitude village—lying between 2000-3000 m above sea level, remote, inaccessible with a large part of its area given over to grazing or lying barren.

Health and the lack of proper health care facilities formed the over riding concern of all three groups of participants. While the local people stressed the problem of unemployment in the area, the researcher felt that illiteracy and lack of awareness were more important.

Education was the first ranking female concern, also listed by the researcher, though with a lower priority. The male participants did not list education among their priorities, but stressed the need for better communication facilities, basic amenities like electricity and a fair price shop as also agricultural inputs like the provision of seedlings. Women listed a veterinary hospital among their priorities, as animal rearing probably falls to their lot. As was

TABLE 5.6: **Village Kathiyan: Priority Areas**

Sl. No.	Male	Female	Researcher
1.	Unemployment	Education	Illiteracy
2.	Communication	Health	Awareness
3.	Health	Unemployment	Health (Poor facilities)
4.	Electricity	Fodder	Education (non-availability of teachers)
5.	Fair Price Shop	Fuel	
6.	Seedlings for horticulture	Veterinary hospital	Marketing

found elsewhere in the study areas, fodder and fuel were emphasised by women, but not perceived by the other participants.

Gender Priorities

Analysing the responses of women from the six PRA exercises held in the region (Table 5.7), it is evident that gender-specific analysis does generate a variant response pattern. While the emphasis on health, the lack of medical facilities especially, maternity and child care centres, and education follows the general response pattern, the universal female emphasis on the problems of fuelwood and fodder collection as mentioned above, is totally unperceived by the male participants as well as the researcher. The need for toilets, the problems of finance for marriages, the requirement for a veterinary hospital are other priorities defined by women, but completely overlooked by men.

Male Priorities

Unemployment, the lack of roads and health care facilities are the top male priority. Priority areas exclusively listed by the male villagers include the provision of electricity, drinking water supply, banking facilities and fair price shops. Surprisingly, women do not rate drinking water or electricity in their list of priorities. Health, education and accessibility continue to remain

TABLE 5.7: **Responses of Women from the Six PRA Exercises**

Sl. No.	Village	Female Priorities					
		1	2	3	4	5	6
1.	Atal	Education	Unemployment	Fuelwood	Health	Marriage expenditure	Fodder
2.	Eithan	Toilets	Health	Education	Fuelwood	Fodder	Roads
3.	Haja-Dasau	Health	Education	Cottage industries	Toilets	Fuelwood	Fodder
4.	Quansi	Health	Unemployment	Toilets	Education	Irrigation	
5.	Sawada	Fodder	Fuelwood	Health	Toilets	Unemployment	Education
6.	Kathiyan	Education	Health	Unemployment	Fodder	Fuelwood	Veterinary hospital

TABLE 5.8: **Responses of Male from the Six PRA Exercises**

Sl. No.	Village	Male priorities					
		1	2	3	4	5	6
1.	Atal	Unemployment	Accessibility	Health	Education	Communication	Water supply
2.	Eithan	Health	Education	Inputs for Horticulture	Electricity	Roads	Bank
3.	Haja-Dasau	Roads	Health	Unemployment	Education	Irrigation	Electricity
4.	Quansi	Health	Roads	Education	Water supply	Irrigation	Agricultural infrastructure
5.	Sawada	Roads	Electricity	Water supply	Education	Bank	Irrigation
6.	Kathiyan	Unemployment	Communication	Health	Electricity	Fair price shop	Horticulture

overriding concerns (Table 5.8).

Researcher's Priorities

From the researchers' point of view, health, particularly the lack of medical facilities, illiteracy, unemployment and lack of awareness are the top priority concerns in the region. The researcher also emphasised the need for marketing and storage facilities and agricultural extension programmes which the villagers did not perceive (Table 5.9).

Felt Needs of the Population

A simple method of estimating the importance of each of the various priority areas listed in the six centres, where the PRA exercise took place, is followed here.

For any one item, there can be a reference of 18 mentions (for each of the six village meetings, three groups participated—men, women and the researcher i.e. a total of 6 × 3 =18). The method involves totalling the number of times the item has been listed among the first-six priorities of each of the participant groups and then calculating the percentage of this to the maximum possible times it can be listed i.e. 18.

e.g., in the case of education/illiteracy.

number of times 'education/illiteracy' has been listed = 16

maximum possible number of times it can be listed = 18

Priority Index = 16/18 × 100 = 88.89 per cent

From Tables 5.7, 5.8 and 5.9, a list of 12 priority items all of which have been listed by at least two groups, has been made. The Felt Needs Index for each of these items has been calculated (Table 5.10).

Similar calculations have been made for each of the priorities listed in the Table using only the villager's ratings and then only the researcher's ratings. (Calculations are made to the base of

TABLE 5.9: **Researcher's Priorities**

Sl. No.	Village	Researcher's priorities					
		1	2	3	4	5	6
1.	Atal	Unemployment	Education	Health			
2.	Eithan	Illiteracy	Health (Poor facilities)	Awareness	Education	Marketing	
3.	Haja-Dasau	Health (Poor medical facilities)	Agricultural inputs	Agricultural extension	Marketing	Storage	Roads
4.	Quansi						
5.	Sawada	Awareness	Unemployment	Illiteracy	Roads	Health (Poor facilities)	
6.	Kathiyan	Illiteracy	Awareness	Health (Poor facilities)	Education	Marketing	

TABLE 5.10: **Felt Needs Index**

Sl. No.	Items	All groups	Villagers	Researcher
1.	Education/illiteracy	88.89	91.67	100.00
2.	Health	88.89	91.67	83.33
3.	Unemployment	50.00	58.33	33.33
4.	Roads	38.89	41.67	33.33
5.	Water supply	16.67	25.00	—
6.	Electricity	16.67	25.00	—
7.	Toilets	22.22	33.33	—
8.	Irrigation	22.22	33.33	—
9.	Agricultural inputs	22.22	16.66	16.67
10.	Fuelwood	27.78	41.67	—
11.	Fodder	27.78	41.67	—
12.	Banks	11.11	16.67	—

twelve for Col. 2 and to the base of 6 for Col. 3). As can be seen from the Table, certain problem areas such as lack of education, poor health facilities, the problem of unemployment and the scanty road network are so dominant that they are perceived almost similarly by all the participants in the exercise overriding both area and gender specificities. However, seven of the items prioritised by 11 per cent to 25 per cent of the participants do not find mention in the researcher priorities. Thus it is obvious that planning, even on the basis of extensive field survey, may leave untouched, problems which are very real to the local people.

Composite Priority Index

While Table 5.10 brings out the felt need of the population and also ranks these needs according to the number of participating groups which identified them, thus highlighting the discrepancies between the needs/problem identification made by the researcher/ planner and by the local people, it was felt that an analysis of the priority given to each identified need would be helpful in the planning process.

To estimate the priority attached to each of the needs/ problems listed in Table 5.10, a simple technique was evolved. The steps involved in the calculation were as follows:

Step - I

Taking any one felt need/problem, a list of the ranks assigned to it by each of the participant groups in each village was made e.g. for education, the ranks assigned were:

1, 1, 2, 3, 4, 5, 2, 3, 4, 4, 4, 1, 1, 2, 3, 4, 4.

Step - II

The ranks were then totalled to give a composite score of 48.

Step - III

To standardise the composite score, it was divided by the total number of responses i.e. 48÷17 = 2.82.
Steps I to III were repeated for each of the selected variables.

Step IV

The standardised composite scores for the twelve selected variables were ranked in ascending order to obtain the composite Priority Index (Table 5.11).

The Table reveals a picture quite different from that emerging from Table 5.10. It can be seen from Table 5.11 that, in terms of priority, unemployment ranks highest in the region followed by health and education. The provision of toilets (a need expressed by women) ranks above the demand for roads and electricity. While fuel and fodder found mention in the lists made by women in five out of the six village centres, in terms of priority, both items rank low—ninth and tenth in a list of twelve.

Summing Up

Based on the foregoing analysis, the following conclusions can be drawn:

TABLE 5.11: **Composite Priority Index**

Sl. No.	Felt Needs	Standardised composite score	Priority Index
1.	Unemployment	2.22	1
2.	Health	2.31	2
3.	Education	2.82	3
4.	Provision of toilets	3.00	4
5.	Roads	3.43	5
6.	Electricity	4.00	6
7.	Agricultural/Horticultural inputs	4.25	7
8.	Drinking water supply	4.33	8
9.	Fodder	4.40	9
10.	Fuelwood	4.75	10
11.	Irrigation	5.25	11
12.	Banks	5.50	12

1. There are certain felt needs/problem areas so dominant that they override area/gender/specificities and educational differentials. In this study, the problems of health, illiteracy/education, unemployment and poor road network fall into the category, and have been identified, and emphasised by all three groups of participants.
2. The needs/problems identified by the researcher on the basis of field observations tend to be generalised rather than related to field reality and overlook many of the basic felt needs of the local people.
3. The inclusion of a separate PRA exercise for the village women has highlighted concerns which play a major role in their day-to-day existence, but remain unperceived by observers and even by the local men i.e. the problems of fodder and fuel supply and the need for toilets.
4. If development priorities in the plan could be based on the priorities given by all groups of participants, the planning process would be participatory in the real sense of the term and would, perhaps, have higher chance of success.

THE CASE OF MUSSOORIE: A MOUNTAIN RESORT TOWN

While the previous section dealt with the use of participatory techniques for sustainable development planning as well as for developing indicators to assess sustainability, this section deals with the use of estimation and projection techniques to develop indicators of sustainability at the micro level. The case in question is the mountain resort town of Mussoorie. A rapid spurt in tourism over the last decade has plunged this quiet residential and educational town into the tourist circuit with all its repercussions in the form of seasonal population explosions with the concomitant strain on local infrastructure, and the attendant noise, traffic jams and pollution. An infinitely more dangerous, insidious change in the form of the mushrooming of real estate activity on once forested fragile slopes is also taking place increasing the danger of soil erosion, and resulting in the choking of water sources and land slips.

Assessing the sustainability of such a town must start with an assessment of its carrying capacity. Only then can indicators be developed and benchmarks laid down against which the impacts of growth and development on sustainability can be measured with a view to guiding the development path.

Mussoorie – A Background

The Mussoorie Urban Agglomeration can be classed as a functional region serving not only its own residents and a sharply fluctuating tourist inflow, but also an hinterland of remote, largely inaccessible mountain hamlets. Located at an altitude of about 2,000 metres in the lower Himalayan ranges of Dehradun district, the hill resort of Mussoorie covers an area of 67.75 square kilometres. The Census of India (1991) records a resident population of 29,629 in the Mussoorie Urban Agglomeration, which includes the Municipality and the Cantonment area (Fig.5.2). Many believe that this is an underestimate since enumeration was done in the month of February (Sunrise of March 1 as the reference moment) when a significant proportion of the city population that normally moves down to the plains during the winter had not returned. Besides, often the population figures

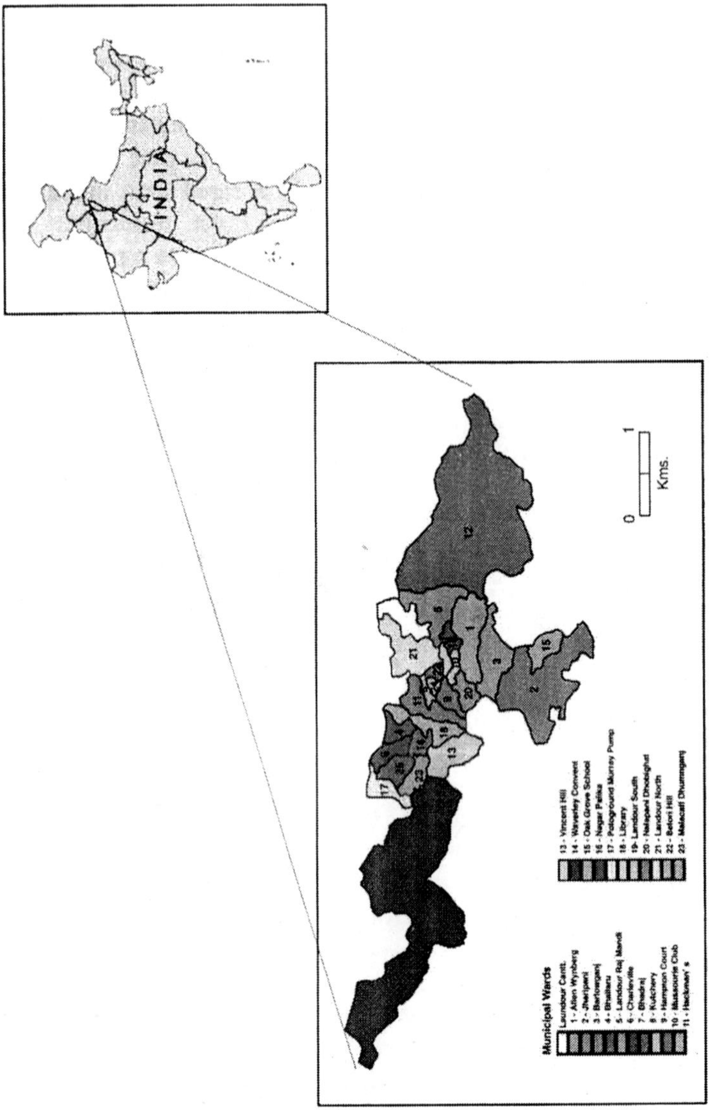

Fig. 5.2 : Mussoorie Urban Agglomeration : Location and Municipal Wards

quoted ignore a substantial number of children studying in the boarding schools of the city, population in the Tibetan settlements, etc. While the Census figures suggest a fluctuating, but sedate growth of population of the city, the tourist inflow has been rising far more rapidly over the years, wherein during the summers the floating population can be as high as twice the permanent population. Public resource allocation for city infrastructure development generally takes into account the number of permanent population. Like all resort towns, the seasonal influx of tourists overloads an already overburdened city infrastructure. As the mainstay of the town is the tourist industry, any plan for sustaining the town, must of necessity, build-in the demand for tourist facility of which the real estate factor is a component. Such a plan must also project future demands of tourism and lay down guidelines for encouraging the industry while sustaining the resource base and environment. It is also to be noted that there is a circular causation between tourism and the environment – unrestrained flow of tourists beyond the city's capacity, with the concomitant strain on the infrastructure and the environment would result in a deteriorating environment and a reduction in the tourist flow. The available information base is rather weak, even with reference to such basic data as population figures.

The main objective of this section is to (a) develop indicators for monitoring carrying capacity and estimating the population carrying capacity of the Mussoorie Urban agglomeration with special reference to available infrastructure; and (b) identify and define benchmarks of various indicators to monitor the carrying capacity of the Mussoorie hills.

Population of Mussoorie

The sustainability of a region is a product of its carrying capacity. Assessing the carrying capacity of an urban eco-system, as a whole or part thereof, is essentially a function of its population, among other things. The first problem involved in estimating the carrying capacity of the Mussoorie Urban Agglomeration was the paucity of reliable population data. The last census conducted in 1991, as was the previous one conducted in the winter of 1981 (Table 5.12), seemed to have considerably underestimated the population.

TABLE 5.12: **Population of Mussoorie Municipal Board and Cantonment (1981 and 1991)**

	1991	1981
1. Mussoorie U.A.	29,629	18,233
2. Landour Cantonment	2,907	1,910
3. Mussoorie (M.B.)	26,722	16,323

However, a survey conducted by the Mussoorie Water Supply and Sewerage Board in 1983 placed the estimated population at 31,500 with an estimated floating population of 20,200. It appears that while the census figures were underestimates, those of the Water Supply and Sewerage Board were overestimates. This necessitated a different approach to an estimation of current (1997) population on the basis of which projections could be made. The various segments of the population of the Mussoorie Urban Agglomeration have been estimated as follows.

Population of the Municipal Board Area

The voters list for the City Board election (updated in 1995) was acquired. The number of voters registered was 17,770 i.e. equivalent to the 18 plus population. As age-wise population break-up was not available for the Mussoorie U.A., the age-wise population data for a similar hill urban area (Shimla district, Himachal Pradesh) was, therefore, obtained. The proportion of population in the 18 years plus age group was 55 per cent. Taking 17,770 as equivalent to 55 per cent of the population, the total population of area under the jurisdiction of the Mussoorie Municipal Board was estimated at 31,218.

Population of the Cantonment Area

Census figures place the population of Landour Cantonment at 2,907 in 1991. The Landour Cantonment Board has confirmed these figures. The Board indicated an annual increase of approximately 5 persons. On this basis, the population was extrapolated as given in Table 5.13. The Landour Cantonment Board further notified us of a decrease of 150 persons with the closing of the PPCL Corporation during 1997. Thus, the 1997 population estimate works out to 2,787.

TABLE 5.13: **Population Estimates for Landour Cantonment Area**

Year	Population	Year	Population
1991	2,907	1995	2,927
1992	2,912	1996	2,932
1993	2,917	1997	[2,937 - 150] = 2,787
1994	2,922		

Tibetan Population

As the Tibetan population of Mussoorie does not figure in the voters list, the number of Tibetans registered with the Local Intelligence Office, Police Department, Dehradun, was obtained. The Tibetan population above 16 years of age was given as 656. To this figure, we added the number of Tibetan Children studying as day scholars in the two schools for Tibetans in Mussoorie i.e. (1) Central School for Tibetans is 170 and (2) Tibetan Homes School population is 33. The Tibetan population, other than boarders in Tibetan Schools was thus placed at 656 + 203 = 859.

Boarders in Tibetan Schools

The total number of boarders in the two Tibetan schools is as follows: (1) Central School for Tibetans had 493 children and (2) Tibetan Homes School had 1,268 children. The boarders in Tibetan schools was thus placed at 1,761. Boarders in Tibetan schools were assessed separately as their vacation timings are different from the public schools and would have an impact on the month-wise population estimates made later.

Boarders in Public Schools

A survey of all 16 boarding schools in Mussoorie was carried out in order to ascertain the number of children residing in them. The number of boarders in Mussoorie in 1997 was 6,028. As the number of boarding schools in the 1983 survey was also 16, it is assumed that the total number of children in boarding schools would remain around the same figure i.e. 6,028 for the period under study. It is not feasible to project the number of new boarding schools that may be established in the future.

Total Permanent Population Estimates for 1997

Final population estimates for 1997 were arrived at in a disaggregated manner—for the winter months and for the rest of the year. As a fairly substantial proportion of the residents of Mussoorie move down to the plains during the winter i.e. December, January and February, it was felt that separate population estimates should be made for the three winter months and for the remainder of the year. The steps involved in this are:

1. The 1981 Census (which was conducted during winter) places the population of Mussoorie at 18,241. The 1991 Census figures are 29,629 which works out to a growth rate of 6.2 per cent per annum between 1981 and 1991. Based on this growth rate, the Census figures for 1981 were projected to 1983 as follows:

Population of Mussoorie U.A.

1981	—	18,241
1982	—	18,241 + 1,131 = 19,372
1983	—	19,372 + 1,201 = 20,573

2. The projected population figures for 1983 were then compared with the Survey figures for 1983 (Water Supply and Sewerage Board) to estimate the proportion of residents who stay in the U.A throughout winter. The survey of 1983 (in season) estimated the population at 31,398 and that projected on the basis of the Census during winter worked out to 20,573. Thus the proportion of winter population to population during the rest of the year is 65 per cent. Thus the total resident population is placed at 23,486 (i.e. 65 per cent of 36,132 in 1997).

3. Following from the above calculations, the population estimates for the winter months (1997) are detailed below:

December and February:
Resident population (22,662) + Boarders in Tibetan Schools (1,761) = 24,423

January:
Resident population (22,662) + Boarders in SOS children's village (1,268) = 23,930

4. The estimates of in-season population are as follows:

Total residents	34,864
Boarders in public schools	4,267
Tibetan boarders	1,761
Total	40,892

5. The population in winter and the rest of the year (1997) is thus estimated to be:

December	24,423
January	23,930
February	*24,423*
Other Months	40,892

Population Projections

Based on the population estimates for 1997, an attempt has been made to project the population for the next twenty-four years i.e. to the year 2021. This was done with a view to estimating the carrying capacity of Mussoorie with reference to essential elements of the infrastructure such as water supply, waste disposal, availability of beds for tourists, etc. Population projections have been made at five-year intervals from 1997 to 2021.

Estimating the Population Growth Rate

Census data for the population of the Mussoorie U.A. was collected for a period of 90 years i.e. for the census years beginning from 1901 at a ten-year interval to 1991. The figures were plotted on a graph and trend lines were fitted—both linear and logarithmic (Figure 5.3). The major difficulty in projecting the population of

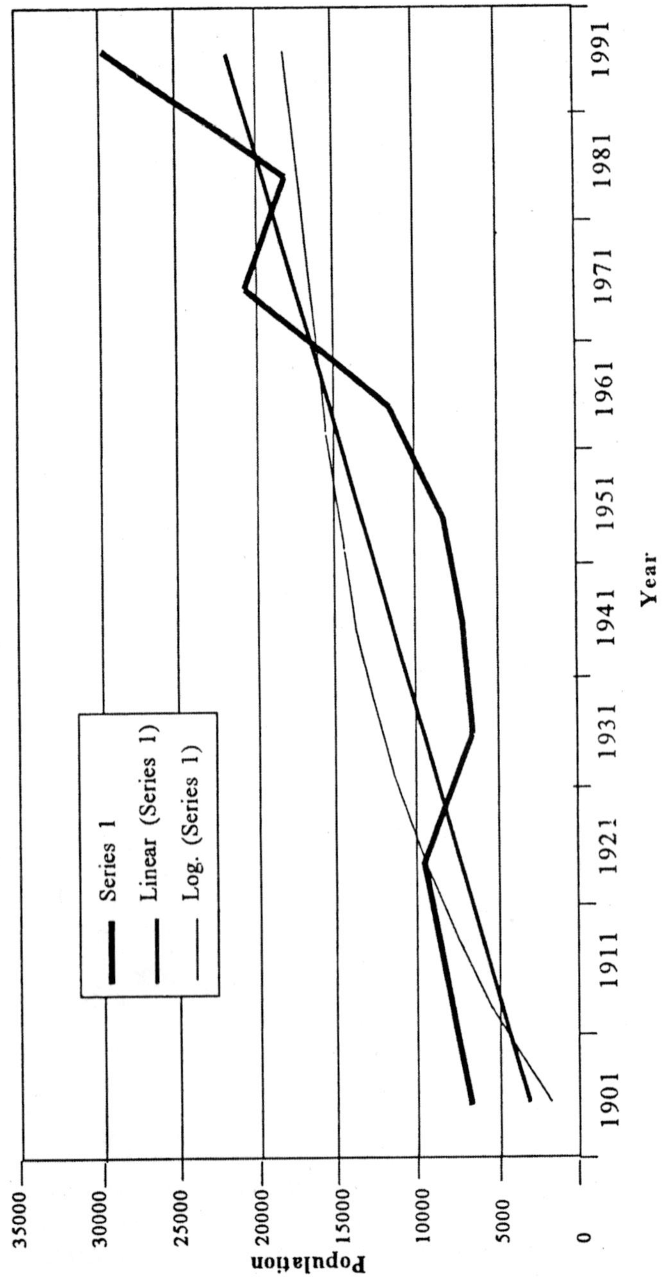

Fig. 5.3: Mussoorie: Population Growth

Mussoorie arises from the fact that during the period of nearly a century under consideration there have been several sharp dips or falls in population (Table 5.14), and the decadal growth rate has been fluctuating correspondingly.

Based on the linear trend line—best fitting the population distribution—over the period 1901-1991, the expected population for the year 1997 was 24,737. On the basis of our own population estimates for 1997 detailed above, the winter population varies between 24,737 and 25,247 which closely approximates the forecast based on the linear trend line. However, to estimate the growth rate of the population, several calculations were made, before adopting what seemed the most realistic figure.

Method I. The growth rate of Mussoorie U.A. between Census 1991 and Census 1981 was calculated as follows:

$$\frac{\text{Pop. 91 (29,629) - Pop. 81 (18,233)}}{\text{Pop. 81 (18,233)}} \times 100$$

= 62.50 per cent (6.25 per cent per annum)

Method II. The growth rate based on the linear trend line is as follows:

Population 2001	= 25,263
Population 1997	= 24,737
Growth rate for 4 years	= 2.13 per cent
Growth rate per year	= 0.53 per cent

Method III. The growth rate based on Survey 1983 and our estimate 1997

Population 1997	= 34,864 (Mussoorie U.A.)
Survey 1983	= 25,456 (Mussoorie U.A.)
Growth rate for 14 years	= 36.96
Growth rate per year	= 2.6 per cent

Method IV. The growth rate based on Survey 1983 and Census 1991

TABLE 5.14: Mussoorie Urban Agglomeration- Population Growth (1901-91)

Name	Population and Growth and Rate									
	1901	1911	1921	1931	1941	1951	1961	1971	1981	1991
Mussoorie U.A	6,461	8,052	9,702	6,116	7,172	8,550	11,238	20.389	18.233	29.629
		(24.62)	(24.49)	(-36.96)	(17.27)	(19.21)	(31.44)	(81.43)	(-10.57)	(62.50)
(i) Landour	1,720	1,500	1,405	1,150	1,206	1,417	1,389	2,351	1,910	2,907
Cantonment		(-12.79)	(-6.33)	(-18.15)	(4.87)	(17.50)	(-1.98)	(69.26)	(-18.76)	(52.20)
(ii) Mussoorie M.B	4,741	6,552	8,297	4,966	5,966	7,133	9,849	18,038	16,323	26,722
		(38.20)	(26.63)	(-40.15)	(20.14)	(19.56)	(38.08)	(83.15)	(-9.51)	(63.71)

Note: Figures in parentheses indicate per cent decadal growth.

Population 1991	= 29,629
Survey 1983	= 25,456
Growth rate for 8 years	= 16.39 per cent
Growth rate per year	= 2.05 per cent

Of the four different growth rates, growth rate I, i.e. 6.25 per cent is unrealistically high while that based on the linear trend is too low. Thus, growth rates three and four were selected and two separate scenarios were generated:

Scenario I based on a growth rate of 2.05 per cent per annum
Scenario II based on a growth rate of 2.60 per cent per annum

Estimating the Growth Rate of Tourists

In order to project the number of tourists visiting Mussoorie over the next 25 years, data on the number of tourists - both Indian and Foreign - entering Mussoorie every month for the years 1990 to 1996 was collected from the Department of Tourism, Government of Uttar Pradesh (see Appendix 5.2). The growth rate of the number of tourists visiting Mussoorie was then calculated as follows:

$$\frac{\text{Number of tourists (1996)—Number of tourists (1990)}}{\text{Number of Tourists (1990)}}$$

Which gives an annual growth rate of 0.6 per cent.

The number of tourists expected to visit the U.A. at five yearly intervals was then calculated on an annual growth rate of 0.6 per cent. Thus, the projection of various segments of Mussoorie Population is given in Table 5.15.

Estimating the Population Pressure

Once the population projections for the different segments of population i.e. permanent population, boarders in residential schools and tourists were made, the next step involved estimating the population pressure on the town. As Mussoorie, being a tourist

TABLE 5.15: **Population Projections for Mussoorie U.A. 1997-2021**

Year	Permanent Population Scenario I Annual Growth Rate : 2.05 Per cent	Permanent Population Scenario II Annual Growth Rate : 2.6 Per cent	Tourists Annual Growth Rate 0.6 Per cent	Boarders in Residential Schools
1997	34,864	34,864	14,27,514	6,028
2001	37,723	38,490	14,61,774	6,028
2006	41,590	43,494	15,05,627	6,028
2011	45,853	49,148	15,50,796	6,028
2016	50,553	55,537	15,97,320	6,028
2021	55,735	62,757	16,45,240	6,028

town, shows sharp seasonal fluctuations in population, it was decided to estimate population pressure on a monthly basis. This would also aid in estimating requirements of water, waste disposal, hotel beds, etc., on a month to month basis.

For each of the selected years, population projections were made on the basis of the two growth rates selected—2.05 per cent per annum for Scenario I and 2.6 per cent per annum for Scenario II.

Permanent Population Estimates

Based on the projected permanent population figure for any particular year, the total in-season permanent population was derived by adding to the permanent population, the total boarders in residential schools. Off-season in Mussoorie coincides with the winter months of December, January and February. The method of estimating the permanent population for these three months is as follows:

For December and February

1. Resident population (65 per cent of the permanent population + all boarders in Tibetan schools), e.g. for

January 1997:

Resident population = 65 per cent of 34,864
= 22,662 + 1761 = 24,423

For January

Resident population (65 per cent of the permanent population + boarders in SOS children's village who stay in Mussoorie throughout the year.

Resident population = 65 per cent of the 34,864
= 22,662 + 1268 = 23,930

Estimates of Tourist Pressure

Based on the average arrival of tourists month-wise from 1990 to 1996, the proportion of tourists arriving in any one month of the year to the total tourists arriving annually was calculated (Table 5.16).

The projected figures for the year 1997, 2001 and 2021 were then split proportionately into tourist arrivals per month. As the average tourist spends 3 days in Mussoorie in May and June and 2 days in the other months, tourist arrivals per month were converted into the number of tourist days. The final figure of tourist pressure was obtained by dividing the number of tourist days per month by the number of days in the month to obtain the number of tourists per day in that particular month as illustrated below:

e.g. To estimate tourist pressure for January 1997

1. Total tourist arrival in January = 45,758
2. Tourist days @ 2 per tourist = 91,516
3. Tourists per day = 91,156/31= 2,952

Final Estimates of Population Pressure

To obtain the final estimates of population pressure per month, the permanent population for each month was added to the tourists, per day in the month (See Appendix 5.3).

TABLE 5.16: **Tourists in-flow to Mussoorie (1990-96)**

Year	Average Indian Tourists (1990-96)	Average Foreign Tourists (1990-96)	Average All Tourists (1990-96)	All Tourists as per cent of Total of Column (4)
1	2	3	4	5
January	3,60,372	50	51,532	3.6
February	4,56,536	76	65,295	4.6
March	6,38,536	143	91,362	6.4
April	8,63,634	145	1,23,521	8.7
May	9,77,264	161	1,63,038	11.5
June	17,55,263	140	2,81,017	19.8
July	13,23,500	165	2,74,081	19.3
August	4,75,000	144	79,310	5.6
September	4,09,000	166	68,332	4.8
October	5,00,000	128	83,461	5.9
November	4,37,000	102	72,935	5.1
December	4,07,000	75	67,908	4.8

Carrying Capacity with Reference to Basic Needs

This section attempts to estimate the carrying capacity of the Mussoorie Urban Agglomeration with respect to basic needs such as water, power, waste disposal, availability of hospital beds, housing, hotel beds for tourists, etc. The methodology followed here is a simple one—of projecting month-wise demands for each amenity as a function of the per capita requirement and the population projected for that month. As the current supply of the amenity is known, anticipating shortfalls in supply in the future becomes simple.

Projected Demand for Water

Water requirements for the U.A. have been worked out on the basis of 150 lpcd (litres per capita per day as given by the office of the Executive Engineer, Uttar Pradesh Jal Nigam, Dehradun). Tables 5.17 and 5.18 give the month-wise breakup of water requirement under the two scenarios. The total available supply as of 1997 is 7 million litres per day. As can be seen from Table 5.17, even at present (1997) the available water supply is sufficient only for the three winter months of December, January and February. By June the demand for water is already 1.5 times the available supply. Under Scenario I (Table 5.17), the situation with respect to monthly demand for water remains the same with sufficient water supply being available from December to February even in the year 2021. However, the peak demand for water in the month of June i.e. 141.5 million litres is more than twice the city's carrying capacity. In fact, for all nine months of the year, from March to November, water demand exceeds the city's supply by about 1.5 times.

TABLE 5.17: **Projected Water Demand @ 150 lpcd (Scenario I)**

Months	1997	2001	2021
January	40,86,750	43,73,450	61,97,550
February	43,66,950	46,62,600	65,09,250
March	**70,17,900**	**70,18,050**	**1,02,83,400**
April	**73,75,800**	**78,34,350**	**1,06,95,750**
May	**85,16,850**	**89,45,700**	**1,20,10,950**
June	**1,03,73,550**	**1,09,04,100**	**1,41,50,850**
July	**88,00,050**	**92,92,800**	**1,23,37,350**
August	69,07,350	**73,30,500**	**1,01,56,050**
September	68,19,000	**72,64,350**	**1,00,54,200**
October	69,48,900	**73,97,250**	**1,02,03,750**
November	68,61,750	**73,08,150**	**1,01,03,550**
December	43,26,600	46,21,200	64,62,600

Current Supply is 70,00,000 lpcd.; Bold figures indicate demand in excess of current supply.

Current carrying capacity = 46,666

Coming to Scenario II (Table 5.18), it is clear that while the existing water supply remains adequate for the period December to February till the year 2016, by the year 2021, water demands in December and February exceed the available supply and the supply in January is just barely adequate to meet the demand generated. The peak demand in June will be about twice the current supply.

TABLE 5.18: **Projected Water Demand @ 150 lpcd (Scenario II)**

Months	1997	2001	2021
January	40,86,750	44,52,150	68,82,150
February	43,66,950	47,37,300	**71,93,850**
March	**70,17,900**	**75,83,100**	**1,13,36,700**
April	**73,75,800**	**79,49,400**	**1,17,49,050**
May	**85,16,850**	**90,60,750**	**1,30,64,250**
June	**1,03,73,550**	**1,10,19,150**	**1,52,04,150**
July	**88,00,050**	**94,07,850**	**1,33,90,650**
August	69,07,350	**74,45,550**	**1,12,09,350**
September	68,19,000	**73,79,400**	**1,11,07,500**
October	69,48,900	**75,12,300**	**1,12,57,050**
November	68,61,750	**74,23,200**	**1,11,56,850**
December	43,26,600	46,95,900	**71,47,200**

Current Supply is 70,00,000 lpcd.; Bold figures indicate demand in excess of supply.

Current carrying capacity = 46,666

Current Carrying Capacity with reference to Water Supply

The current supply of water in Mussoorie is about 70,00,000 litres per day. Based on a daily per capita requirement of 150 lpcd, the carrying capacity of the Mussoorie Urban Agglomeration is estimated as below:

Available water supply	: 70,00,000 litres per day
Demand per capita	: 150 litres per day
Carrying Capacity	: 46,666 persons

Projected Needs for Waste Disposal

The waste generated in the Mussoorie U.A. was estimated separately for the local population and the tourists. The rates selected were 350 gms. of waste per capita per day for residents and 400 gms. per capita per day for tourists. These estimates were based on trials conducted in Mussoorie during May 1997.

Tables 5.19 and 5.20 show the month-wise generation of waste by the resident population and by the tourists visiting the U.A. In 1997 itself, the Municipality had to cope with a daily waste disposal ranging between 9.7 tonnes in January to 26 tonnes in the peak season (June). By the year 2021, this daily disposal load will be at the minimum, 15 tonnes and in the peak season will touch nearly 35 tonnes under Scenario I. If higher growth rates are assumed (Scenario II), the lowest waste load would be 16 tonnes and the highest over 37 tonnes. The city utilises a single dumping site that could become a health risk, with the chances of polluting the Bhilaru Stream which is an important water source for the area.

Projected Demand for Beds in Hotels

As the economy of the Mussoorie Urban Agglomeration is almost wholly dependent on the tourist trade, it becomes crucial to assess the availability of residential accommodation for tourists. This assessment is normally made on the basis of number of beds available. The Department of Tourism, Mussoorie, provided figures on the beds available in the 140 registered hotels both Government and Private, i.e. 8,028. However, as a large number of tourists visiting Mussoorie are from the lower middle and middle income groups, it is necessary to include other places which offer accommodation on a cheaper basis such as *Gurudwaras* and *Dharamshalas*. Accordingly, all eight Dharamshalas listed in the tourist information brochure were visited and information was collected on the accommodation available. It is estimated that 1,598 beds are available in these institutions for tourists. All the institutions verified that available beds are full during the season i.e. May and June.

A third group providing hospitality to tourists in Mussoorie is the holiday homes of various public sector undertakings and private firms, and paying guest houses run by private individuals.

TABLE 5.19: **Estimates of Waste Generation in Mussoorie (Scenario I)**

Months	1997			2001			2021		
	Permanent Pop. @ 350 gm/cap. (kg)	Tourists per day @ 400 gm/cap (kg)	Total	Permanent Pop. @ 350 gm/cap. (kg)	Tourists per day @ 400 gm/cap (kg)	Total	Permanent Pop. @ 350 gm/cap (kg)	Tourists per day @ 400 gm/cap (kg)	Total
January	8,375	1,326	9,701	9,026	1,358	10,384	13,124	1,528	14,652
February	8,548	1,876	10.424	9,198	1,921	11,119	13,296	2,162	15,458
March	14,312	1,958	16,270	15,313	2,414	17,727	21,617	2,717	24,334
April	14,312	3.312	17.624	15,313	3,391	18,704	21,617	3.817	25,434
May	14,312	6,355	20,667	15.313	6,355	21.668	21,617	7,324	28.941
June	14,312	11,306	25,618	15,313	11,577	26,890	21,617	13,030	34,647
July	14,312	7,110	21,422	15,313	7,280	22.593	21.617	8,194	29.811
August	14,312	2,063	16,375	15,313	2,028	17,361	21,617	2,378	23,995
September	14,312	1,827	16,139	15,313	1,871	17,184	21,617	2,106	23,723
October	14,312	2,174	16,486	15,313	2,226	17,539	21,617	2,505	24,122
November	14,312	1,941	16,253	15.313	1,988	17,301	21,617	2,238	23,855
December	8,548	1,768	10,316	9,198	1,810	11,008	13,296	2.038	15,334

@ 400 gms/capita/day (for tourists) and 350 gms/capita/day (for permanent population).

TABLE 5.20: **Waste Generation (Scenario II)**

Months	1997			2001			2021		
	Permanent Pop. @ 350 gm/cap. (kg)	Tourists per day @ 400 gm/cap (kg)	Total	Permanent Pop. @ 350 gm/cap. (kg)	Tourists per day @ 400 gm/cap (kg)	Total	Permanent Pop. @ 350 gm/cap (kg)	Tourists per day @ 400 gm/cap (kg)	Total
January	8,375	1,326	9,701	9,200	1,358	10,558	14,721	1,528	16,249
February	8,548	1,876	10,424	9,373	1,921	11,294	14.894	2,162	17,056
March	14,312	1.958	16,270	15,581	2,414	17,995	24.075	2,717	26.792
April	14,312	3,312	17,624	15,581	3,391	18,972	24.075	3,817	27,892
May	14.312	6,355	20,667	15,581	6,355	21,936	24,075	7,324	31,399
June	14,312	11,306	25,618	15,581	11,577	27,158	24,075	13,030	37,105
July	14,312	7,110	21,422	15,581	7,280	22,861	24,075	8,194	32,269
August	14,312	2,063	16,375	15,581	2,048	17,629	24,075	2.378	26,453
September	14,312	1,827	16.139	15,581	1,871	17,452	24,075	2,106	26.181
October	14,312	2,174	16,486	15,581	2,226	17,801	24,075	2,505	26,580
November	14,312	1,941	16,253	15,581	1,988	17,569	24,075	2,238	26,313
December	8,548	1,768	10,316	9,373	1,811	11,184	14.894	2,038	16.932

A survey of these revealed an additional availability of 218 beds. The total estimated availability of beds for tourists in Mussoorie is given in Table 5.21.

TABLE 5.21: **Beds available for Tourists in Mussoorie**

1.	Beds in 140 registered hotels	8,028
2.	Beds in 8 *Gurudwaras, Dharamshalas, Musafirkhanas* and Temples	1,598
3.	Beds in holiday homes and paying guest houses	218
	Total Beds available	9,844

Table 5.22 shows the daily arrival of tourists in Mussoorie in each month. It is obvious that during the season, i.e. in the months of April, May and June, the number of incoming tourists is much greater than the accommodation available in the city. Thus, while in May and July, only 62 per cent and 55 per cent of the arriving tourists can be accommodated, in June, 65 per cent have to return the same day because of lack of accommodation. Thus, while the city bears the burden of providing water and other facilities to these incoming tourists, the regular traffic jams, resulting emission of pollutants, and the responsibility of disposing of the waste generated, it still loses out on the income which would accrue to the town if the tourists spent the night. This would also, perhaps, reduce the constant traffic jams as the day tourists rush to get back to Dehradun before nightfall. On the other hand, there is a considerable excess capacity during several months in the year.

By 2021, 70 per cent of the tourists arriving in Mussoorie in June would be forced to return to Dehradun or to proceed beyond Mussoorie in search of accommodation. The vast potential in the tourist trade opens up several possibilities—that of increasing the capacity of existing hotels, granting licenses to new hotels which has to be viewed in the context of excess capacity during off season, or boosting the development of alternative locations like Dhanaulti or Chakrata. This would also necessitate augmenting access to such alternative centres.

Current Carrying Capacity with reference to Tourism

As the total number of beds for tourists in all hotels, guesthouses

TABLE 5.22: **Tourist Flow Per Day—Estimates (Mussoorie)**

	1997	2001	2021
January	3,315	3,395	3,821
February	4,690	4,803	5,406
March	5,894	6,036	6,793
April	8,280	8,478	9,542
May	**15,887**	**16,810**	**18,310**
June	**28,265**	**28,943**	**32,576**
July	**17,775**	**18,201**	**20,486**
August	5,157	5,119	5,944
September	4,568	4,678	5,265
October	5,434	5,564	6,262
November	4,853	4,970	5,594
December	4,421	4,527	5,095

Current Carrying Capacity for overnight tourists is 9,844. Bold figures indicate demand in excess of supply.

and *dharamshalas* in the town amounts to 9,844, the current carrying capacity of the town with reference to overnight tourists is 9,844.

Projected Demand for Hospital Beds

Town planning norms in India place the requirement of hospitals at one general hospital per 50,000 population. As Mussoorie has 3 hospitals with capacities ranging from 30 to 53 beds, it was decided that a more appropriate measure would be the availability of hospital beds against basic requirements. The fourth—the Northern Railway Hospital at Jhari Pani—has a 58-bed facility. However, it caters to railway personnel only and has thus been excluded from the carrying capacity estimates. In order to estimate the requirement for hospital beds, one of the largest general hospitals in Dehradun i.e. the Doon Hospital with a capacity of 232 beds was selected. At the rate of one general hospital for

50,000 persons specified by the MDDA as well as Indian town planning norms, the requirement for hospital beds works out to one bed for a population of 215 persons. Thus it was decided to adopt the norm of one hospital bed per 200 persons, as the basis of working out the carrying capacity of Mussoorie with reference to health facilities. The number of hospital beds available in Mussoorie in 1997 is detailed in Table 5.23.

TABLE 5.23: **Availability of Hospital Beds in Mussoorie (1997)**

Sl. No.	Name of Hospital	Number of Beds
1.	St. Mary's Hospital, Mussoorie	53
2.	Civil Hospital, Mussoorie	30
3.	Community Hospital, Landour	50
4.	Private Nursing Homes	20
	Total (Beds)	153

Projected requirements for hospital beds even under Scenario I (Table 5.24) reveal a shortage of beds from March to November. In fact, even at present (1997), the shortfall in hospital beds in the peak month of June is as much as 193. The pattern remains the same over the next twenty years, though the shortfall in the peak season increases sharply to 319 beds implying that the peak demand for hospital beds is over 200 per cent of the supply. While the large boarding schools do have infirmary beds, these cannot be equated to specialised hospital beds, but must be treated at par with home nursing facilities.

By the year 2021, the requirement for hospital beds exceeds the availability throughout the year.

Under Scenario II (Table 5.25) with the higher population growth rate of 2.6 per cent, the shortfall in hospital bed begins as early as 2001 with sufficient beds being available only in the month of January. From the year 2006, the number of beds available is insufficient throughout the year. By 2021, the peak requirement in the months of May, June and July is such that available supply meets only 32-38 per cent of the requirement.

TABLE 5.24: **Requirement of Hospital Beds (Scenario I)**

Month	1997	2001	2021
January	136	146	**207**
February	146	**155**	**217**
March	**234**	**234**	**343**
April	**246**	**261**	**356**
May	**284**	**298**	**400**
June	**346**	**363**	**472**
July	**293**	**310**	**411**
August	**230**	**244**	**338**
September	**227**	**242**	**335**
October	**232**	**247**	**340**
November	**229**	**244**	**337**
December	144	**154**	**215**

Availability of Hospital Beds–153. Current Carrying Capacity = 30,600 persons. Bold figures indicate demand in excess of supply.

TABLE 5.25: **Requirement of Hospital Beds (Scenario II)**

	1997	2001	2021
January	136	148	**229**
February	146	**158**	**240**
March	**234**	**253**	**378**
April	**246**	**265**	**392**
May	**284**	**302**	**435**
June	**346**	**367**	**507**
July	**293**	**314**	**446**
August	**230**	**248**	**374**
September	**227**	**246**	**370**
October	**232**	**250**	**375**
November	**229**	**247**	**372**
December	144	**156**	**238**

Availability of Hospital Beds–153. Bold figures indicate demand in excess of supply.

Current Carrying Capacity = 30,600 persons

Concluding Observations

On the basis of the above analysis, we may come to some tentative conclusions.

— Firstly, there is the dilemma of the need to protect and strengthen the tourist industry while minimising negative impacts of such growth, manifested in pressure on services and city infrastructure, including water, sanitation, land for housing, power, transportation and congestion.

— Secondly, the study has shown poor and grossly inadequate database on which development activities are planned. It has been argued earlier in this study that there is a need to include temporal considerations in estimating even such basic parameters as population of the city. Often resource allocations are based on per capita basis and in cities like Mussoorie it becomes necessary to estimate tourist population, which in several months in the year far exceeds the resident population.

— Thirdly, based on standard norms and requirements it has been pointed out that:

— The requirement of water far exceeds the availability even at present for nine months of the year, the three months of adequate water supply being in those winter months when a third of the resident population is out of Mussoorie. The projections also show that by the year 2021 current water supply will be inadequate even during the winter months.

— Estimates of waste generation (based on trials conducted separately for resident and tourist population) indicate the vast differences in the waste generated between the peak season and the lean season – with the former recording three times that of the latter. The increase during the next two decades is estimated to be one and half times the present. The fact that tests conducted show that the water quality in and around Mussoorie is within the pollution limits prescribed has been noted. However, with a single dumping ground whose location poses a major threat of polluting one of the important sources of drinking water of the city, waste management remains a problem to be attended to on a priority basis.

— The demand for tourist accommodation is again to be seen in the context of temporal dimension. The supply exceeds the demand by two times during nine months in a year and is likely to be so even in the next quarter of a century, while substantially short during the peak season. The answer obviously, is not in creating/ augmenting capacities in hotels – the problem begs a more innovative solution. One option is to identify other hill towns with better carrying capacity and reasonable access to the plains, for development as eco-tourism centres.

— Medical facilities expressed in terms of availability of hospital beds indicate a short fall even at present during the peak season and is expected to be so throughout the year in the next two decades at the current level of supply. As noted earlier, availability of land will be the limiting factor in expansion of land dependent infrastructure.

APPENDICES

APPENDIX – 5.1

LIST OF VILLAGES REPRESENTED IN THE PRA EXERCISE

Central Place	Village Code	Village Name
1	2	3
Atal	23	Anu
	24	Sainj
	25	Pharij
	26	Atal
	59	Penuwa
	60	Kabakera
	61	Thartha
	62	Pingua
	63	Kunwa
	64	Gorcha
	65	Punig
	66	Kandoi
		Himachal Pradesh
		Sobal
		Bhatgarh Seran
		Bandur
Eithan		
	43	Sarani
	44	Patud
	45	Eithan
Haja-Dasau		
	85	Matiyana
	86	Dasau
	87	Haja
	89	Kritrauli
Quansi (Jogiou)	111	Khatwa

1	2	3
	112	Kharsi
	113	Punaha Pokhri
	114	Siri Barkoti
	116	Bijnu
	117	Virpa
	118	Chunauti
	119	Kandidhar
	120	Jogiou
	121	Thanta
Sawada (Dungri)		
	41	Kistoor
	42	Sunir
	47	Sunoi
	48	Sainj
	49	Kunain
	50	Kholara
	51	Raited
	52	Kharaura
	53	Amrad Jhabarad
	54	Dungri
	55	Bhandroli
	73	Rajanu
Kathiyan (Bhatad)		
	29	Dharmigad
	30	Purdad
	31	Phanar
	32	Bhagoor
	33	Obraser
	34	Bhoot
	35	Dhrinad
	37	Bhated (Bhatar)
	38	Nimga
	39	Kerad

APPENDIX – 5.2

TOURIST INFLOW IN MUSSOORIE

	1990	1991	1992	1993	1994	1995	1996
January	57,372	50,000	60,000	48,000	50,000	45,000	50,000
	44	15	36	27	34	60	132
February	66,536	60,000	70,000	75,000	70,000	55,000	60,000
	64	49	43	38	36	166	138
March	93,536	95,000	1,00,000	1,00,000	90,000	75,000	85,000
	53	71	75	73	135	308	286
April	1,26,301	1,30,333	1,30,000	1,32,000	1,20,000	1,00,000	1,25,000
	—	50	140	234	127	231	236
May	1,82,264	—	2,15,000	1,80,000	1,60,000	1,30,000	1,10,000
	75	124	115	132	219	226	238
June	2,70,263	—	3,25,000	2,60,000	2,80,000	2,50,000	3,00,000
	125	130	109	69	184	256	230

(Contd.)

APPENDIX-5.2: *(Contd.)*

	1990	1991	1992	1993	1994	1995	1996
July	1,58,500	—	2,90,000	2,80,000	2,95,000	3,00,000	3,20,000
	105	138	135	83	154	267	270
August	1,00,000	—	1,25,000	70,000	60,000	55,000	65,000
	140	111	103	68	160	—	280
September	80,000	—	1,21,000	78,000	50,000	60,000	65,000
	114	175	94	95	—	180	220
October	80,000	—	1,55,000	95,000	15,000	80,000	75,000
	174	115	137	154	110	—	78
November	75,000	—	1,05,000	90,000	35,000	60,000	72,000
	51	63	105	104	105	153	136
December	80,000	—	60,000	65,000	40,000	70,000	92,000
	29	28	32	99	120	—	140
TOTAL	13,69,772	15,00,000	17,56,000	14,73,000	12,20,000	12,80,000	14,19,000
	1041	1069	1127	1176	1384	1847	2423

Note: The first row represents Indian Tourists and the second represents foreign tourists. (—) represents absence of data.

APPENDIX – 5.3

MONTH-WISE VARIATION IN POPULATION PRESSURE-1997

Months	Permanent Population	Number of Tourists	Tourist Days @ 3 for May/ June 2 for other Months	Tourists per day	Pop. pressure per day
January	23,930	51,390	1,02,780	3,315	27,245
February	24,423	65,666	1,31,332	4,690	29,113
March	40,892	91.361	1,82,722	5,894	46,786
April	40,892	1,24.194	2,48,388	8,280	49,172
May	40,892	1.64.164	4,92,492	15,887	56,779
June	40,892	2.82,648	8,47,944	28,265	69,157
July	40,892	2,75.510	5,51,020	17.775	58,667
August	40,892	79.941	1,59,882	5,157	46,049
September	40,892	68,521	1,37,042	4,568	45,460
October	40,892	82,223	1,68.446	5,434	46,326
November	40,892	71,803	1,45,606	4,853	45,745
December	25,247	68,521	1,37,042	4,421	28,844

In Season Population

Total Residents = 34.864

Boarders in Public Schools = 4,267

Boarders in Tibetan Schools = 1,761

Total = 40,892

Winter Population

December and February

65 per cent of residents (22.662)+
Boarders in Tibetan Schools (1,761)
= 24,423

January

65 per cent of residents (22,662) +
Children in SOS
Children's Village (1,268) = 22,930

SCENARIO I

MONTH-WISE VARIATION IN POPULATION PRESSURE - 2001

Months	Permanent Population	Number of Tourists	Tourist Days @ 3 for May/ June 2 for other Months	Tourists per day	Pop. pressure per day
January	25,788	52,624	1,05,248	3,395	29,183
February	26,281	67,242	1,34,484	4,803	31,084
March	43,751	93,553	1,87,106	6,036	46,787
April	43,751	1,27,174	2,54,348	8,478	52,229
May	43,751	1,64,164	4,92,492	15,887	59,638
June	43,751	2,89,431	8,68,293	28,943	72,694
July	43,751	2,82,122	5,64,244	18,201	61,952
August	43,751	79,339	1,58,678	5,119	48,870
September	43,751	70,165	1,40,330	4,678	48,429
October	43,751	86,245	1,72,490	5,564	49,315
November	43,751	74,550	1,49,100	4,970	48,721
December	26,281	70,165	1,40,330	4,527	30,808

In Season Population

Total Residents = 37,723

Boarders in Public Schools = 4,267

Boarders in Tibetan Schools = 1,761

Total = 43,751

Winter Population

December and February

65 per cent of residents (24,520)+

Boarders in Tibetan Schools (1,761)

= 26,281

January

65 per cent of residents (24,520) +
Children in SOS Children's Village
(1,268) = 25,788

SCENARIO I

MONTH-WISE VARIATION IN POPULATION PRESSURE - 2021

Months	Permanent Population	Number of Tourists	Tourist Days @ 3 for May/ June 2 for other Months	Tourists per day	Pop. pressure per day
January	37,496	59,229	1,18,458	3,821	41,317
February	37,989	75,681	1,51,362	5,406	43,395
March	61,763	1,05,295	2,10,590	6,793	68,556
April	61,763	1,43,136	2,86,271	9,542	71,305
May	61,763	1,89,203	5,67,609	18,310	80,073
June	61,763	3,25,757	9.77,271	32,576	94,339
July	61,763	3,17,531	6,35,062	20,486	82,249
August	61,763	92,133	1,84,266	5,944	67,707
September	61,763	78,971	1,57,942	5,265	67,028
October	61,763	97,069	1,94,138	6,262	68,025
November	61,763	83,907	1,67,814	5,594	67,357
December	37,989	78,971	1,57,942	5,095	43,084

In Season Population

Total Residents = 55,735

Boarders in Public Schools = 4,267

Boarders in Tibetan Schools = 1,761

Total = 61,763

Winter Population

December and February

65 per cent of residents (36,228)+

Boarders in Tibetan Schools (1,761)

= 37,989

January

65 per cent of residents (36,228) + Children in SOS Children's Village (1,268) = 34,496

SCENARIO II

MONTH-WISE VARIATION IN POPULATION PRESSURE - 2001

Months	Permanent Population	Number of Tourists	Tourist Days @ 3 for May/ June 2 for other Months	Tourists per day	Pop. pressure per day
January	26,286	52,624	1,05,248	3,395	**29,681**
February	26,779	67,242	1,34,484	4,803	**31,582**
March	44,518	93,553	1,87,106	6,036	**50,554**
April	44,518	1,27,174	2,54,348	8,478	**52,996**
May	44,518	1,64,164	4,92,492	15,887	**60,405**
June	44,518	2,89,431	8,68,293	28,943	**73,461**
July	44,518	2,82,122	5,64,244	18,201	**62,719**
August	44,518	79,339	1,58,678	5,119	**49,637**
September	44,518	70,165	1,40,330	4,678	**49,196**
October	44,518	86,245	1,72,490	5,564	**50,082**
November	44,518	74,550	1,49,100	4,970	**49,488**
December	26,779	70,165	1,40,330	4,527	**31,306**

In Season Population

Total Residents = 38,490

Boarders in Public Schools = 4,267

Boarders in Tibetan Schools = 1,761

Total = 44,518

Winter Population

December and February

65 per cent of residents (25,018)+ Boarders in Tibetan Schools (1,761) = 26,779

January

65 per cent of residents (25,018) + Children in SOS Children's Village (1,268) = 26,286

SCENARIO II

MONTH-WISE VARIATION IN POPULATION PRESSURE - 2021

Months	Permanent Population	Number of Tourists	Tourist Days @ 3 for May/ June 2 for other Months	Tourists per day	Pop. pressure per day
January	42,060	59,229	1,18,458	3,821	45,881
February	42,553	75,681	1,51,362	5,406	47,959
March	68,785	1,05,295	2,10,590	6,793	75,578
April	68,785	1,43,136	2,86,272	9,542	78,327
May	68,785	1,89,203	5,67,669	18,310	87,095
June	68,785	3,25,757	9,77,271	32,576	1,01,361
July	68,785	3,17,531	6,35,062	20,486	89,271
August	68,785	92,133	1,84,266	5,944	74,729
September	68,785	78,971	1,57,942	5,265	74,050
October	68,785	97,069	1,94,138	6,262	75,047
November	68,785	93,907	1,67,814	5,594	74,379
December	42,553	78,971	1,57,942	5,095	47,648

In Season Population

Total Residents = 62,757

Boarders in Public Schools = 4,267

Boarders in Tibetan Schools = 1,761

Total = 68,785

Winter Population

December and February

65 per cent of residents (40,792)+

Boarders in Tibetan Schools (1,761)

= 42,553

January

65 per cent of residents (40,792) + Children in SOS Children's Village (1,268) = 42,060

6

SUMMING UP

The study may be viewed as an attempt to develop a set of indicators to measure the relative position of various spatial units (space economies) on the basis of, the now familiar, Quality of Life and Quality of Environment Indicators. It is posited that the nature of indicators and the methods of aggregating them need to change according to the context. The contexts illustrated in this study are – international comparisons, a national economy over a time span, a regional economy, and micro units such as villages and towns.

The selection of indicators for studies at the macro-level is constrained by easy access to and availability of data, whereas at the micro-level much of the indicators required have to be met through generation of primary data. When comparison over time is attempted, the data related problems accentuate, both because of lack of time series data on the selected indicator and changes in definitions, on the one hand and changes in the boundaries of spatial units, on the other. The preceding analysis, therefore, chose to use simple methods of constructing composite indices rather than more sensitive methods that call for more refined data sets. An attempt has also been made to combine the QOL and QOE indices in order to rank various spatial units on a scale of sustainable development. However, such an index is beset with problems of interpretation, since the indicators have been given equal weights. As a result, a high index value may compensate for poor quality of environment and *vice versa* leading to distorted ranking. Plotting QOL and QOE scores of various observations in a scattergram could unravel this distortion.

Notwithstanding such methodological and data problems, based on the above analysis, broad conclusions on indices for monitoring sustainability may be drawn.

Cross country comparisons of indices of QOL and QOE bring out the fact that it is possible to achieve higher quality of life, without necessarily losing out on the status of environment, as evidenced by Malaysia and Thailand. On the contrary, there are also situations such as Bhutan and Bangladesh, where the countries are relatively worse off on both dimensions – underlining the fact that low quality of life does not ensure better quality of environment. In this context, it is necessary to realise that macro comparisons can sometimes be misleading. For one, large countries may obtain their development scores from certain pockets and environmental status from others. Secondly, the indicators, particularly of environmental quality, have to be relevant to the entire study area, in the absence of which, the results remain open to question. For example, the probability of the incidence of forest cover in the countries of the Middle East is insignificant, compared to tropical and semi-tropical countries and as such, if area under forest is taken as an indicator of environmental quality, the countries of the Middle East would stand to lose out on this dimension.

Time series analysis of indices of QOL and QOE pertaining to India indicates the possibility of significant rise in the quality of life, without rapid deterioration in the status of environment. At the macro level, environmental policies have tended to address mega development projects and environmental considerations, particularly those relating to forests and wildlife, have weighed with the government. The time series analysis also points to the possibility of smaller fluctuations in environmental status as compared to quality of life indicators.

Inter-State comparisons within India, also reinforce the fact that different combinations of status of quality of life and environment are possible and, therefore, appropriate development policies could be framed that could subsume environmental considerations. The analysis has identified States with low status of environmental quality that need to address environmental restoration issues. The study underlines not only the gross inter-State disparities in the quality of life and quality of environment, but also the changes that have taken place during the last five decades of development.

The analysis pertaining to a natural region – The Hindu Kush Himalayas – indicates the influence of State level (administrative unit) policies on the nature of development. The fact that intra-regional disparities exist, within a mountain tract characterised by common anchoring physical conditions, and that such disparities are on the lines of administrative divisions (States) emphasises the relevance of the growth priorities of various States.

At the micro-level, the participatory approach to identification of development problems, points out to the possible gender bias as well as researcher bias in the rural context. The study at the village level also brings out the fact that problems such as the access to education and health facilities and employment opportunities appear to be of greater priority, than issues such as lack of fodder and fuel wood that represent the environmental dimension. Such conditions warrant awareness campaigns on a substantial scale, since, sustainable resource use practices at the household level have far reaching impact on environmental status.

The urban case study, similarly, highlights the dilemma of tourist towns with seasonal fluctuations in conditions and calls for a system of periodic monitoring of key indicators of carrying capacity in order to avoid crisis situations and urban decay.

APPENDIX

DATA SOURCES

For South Asia

1. *World Development Reports* of the World Bank, New York: Oxford University Press. (for the years 1979 to 1997).
2. *Human Development Reports*, United Nations Development Programme, New York: Oxford University Press (for the years 1995 tc 1997).
3. *World Resources*, World Resources Institute, New York: Oxford University Press (for the years 1992-93 and 1994-95).

For India: Country Level

1. Government of India, *Economic Survey*, Ministry of Finance, Statistical Division, (for the years, 1984-85 to 1995-96).
2. Government of India, Basic Statistics Relating to the Indian Economy, 1950-51.

For India: State Level

1. Census of India, 1991-India—State and District level data in floppies (unpublished).
2. Census of India, 1981, Series I, India Part II-A (II) *General Population Tables.*
3. Census of India, 1981, Part II - A and B, *General Economic Tables.*
4. Census of India, 1981, Part IV A, *Social and Cultural Tables.*
5. Census of India, 1971, Series I, India Part II A (II) *General Population Tables.*

6. Census of India, 1961, *Final Population Totals*, Paper no. 1 of 1962.
7. Census of India, 1961, Vol. I Part I-A(II) India – *Levels of Regional Development in India.*
8. Census of India, 1951, Vol. I, Part II C – *Economic Tables.*
9. Census of India, 1951, Vol. I, Part II A – *Demographic Tables.*
10. *Statistical Abstract of India*, Central Statistical Organisation, Department of Statistics, Ministry of Planning, Government of India for the years 1975, 1987, 1989, 1995.
11. *Statistical Outline* of India for the years 1980-81, 1981-82, 1988-89.
12. *Statistical Pocket Book* of the Indian Union for the years 1966 and 1984.
13. *Basic Statistics* Relating to the Indian Economy for the years 1950-51 and 1980-81.
14. *Inter-State Comparative Statistics*, Economics and Statistics Division, State Planning Institute, Lucknow, UP for the years 1989 and 1993.
15. *Know Your State*, Selected Economic Indicators, 1994, Lal Bahadur Shastri National Academy of Administration, Mussoorie, UP.
16. *Sarvekshana*, 1994, January – March.

For the Hindu Kush Himalayan Region

1. Census of India, 1981, Series 22, Uttar Pradesh, Part III – A & B (i), *General Economic Tables.*
2. Census of India, 1981, Series – 7, Himachal Pradesh, Part III – A & B, *General Economic Tables.*
3. Census of India, 1981, Series-7, Himachal Pradesh Part IV – A, *Social and Cultural Tables.*
4. Census of India, 1981, Series – 8, Jammu and Kashmir, Part – III, A & B, Vol. I, *General Economic Tables.*
5. *Agricultural Statistics*, 1982, Department of Agriculture, Government of Uttar Pradesh.
6. *Annual Season and Crop Report*, 1980-81, Government of Himachal Pradesh, Directorate of Land Records.
7. *Indian Agricultural Statistics*, 1977-78 to 1981-82, Jammu

and Kashmir, Directorate of Economics and Statistics, Department of Agriculture and Cooperation, Ministry of Agriculture and Rural Development, New Delhi.

8. *Statistical Abstract, Uttar Pradesh*—1988-89, Economics and Statistics Division, State Planning Institute, Lucknow.
9. *Statistical Outline of Himachal Pradesh*, 1983 and 1985, Directorate of Economics and Statistics, Himachal Pradesh, Simla.
10. *Digest of Statistics*, 1985-86, Government of Jammu and Kashmir, Directorate of Economics and Statistics, Planning and Development Department.

For Chakrata District

Primary data was generated through participatory techniques during field surveys.

For Mussoorie Urban Agglomeration

Data was generated through estimation and projection techniques based on the voters' list and sample surveys.

SELECT BIBLIOGRAPHY

AAAS. (1964) *Agricultural Sciences for the Developing Nations.* Washington, DC: American Association for the Advancement of Sciences 1964.

Abel, N. and Blaikie, P. M. (1986), Elephants, People, Parks and Development: The case of the Luangwa Valley Zambia. *Environmental Management.* 10(6), pp. 735-51.

Adams, W. M. (1990) *Green Development: Environment and Sustainability in the Third World.* London: Routledge.

ADB. (1969), *Regional Seminar on Agriculture: Papers and Proceedings.* Manila: Asian Development Bank.

Adesheshiah, M. S. (ed.) (1990). *Sustainable Development: Its Content, Scope and Prices.* New Delhi: Lancer Publication.

Agarwal, A. (ed.) (1992). *The Price of Forests: Proceedings of a Seminar on the Economics of the Sustainable Use of Forest Resources.* New Delhi: Centre for Science & Environment.

Agarwal, Anil. (1992) *Towards a Green World.* New Delhi: Centre for Science & Environment.

Agarwal, A. and S. Narain. (1991), *Towards Green Villages.* New Delhi: Centre for Science and Environment.

Agarwal, B. *Cold Hearths and Barren Slopes, The Wood Fuel Crisis in the Third World.* London: Zed Books Ltd.

Agarwal, V. P. and S. V. S. Rana. (1985) *Environment and Natural Resources.* New Delhi: Society of Bioscience.

Ahmad Yusuf J., Salah El Serafy and Ernst Lutz. (eds.) (1989) *Environmental Accounting for Sustainable Development.* Washington, DC: World Bank.

Ahmad, J. (1984) *Environmental Decision-Making.* London: Hodder and Stroughton.

Ahmad, Yusuf. J. (1989) *Environmental Accounting for Sustainable Development.* Washington : The World Bank.

AIAF(1969) *An Agricultural Plan for India.* New Delhi: All India Agriculturists Federation.

Alagh, Y.K. (1993) Socio-Economic Structures and Sustainable Agriculture in Stressed Conditions, *Indian Journal of Public Administration* 39(3); July-Sept., p. 441.

Alfsen, K.H., Bye, T. and Lorentson, L. (1987) *National Resource Accounting and Analysis, the Norwegian Experience 1978-1986.* Oslo: Central Bureau of Statistics.

Allenby. (1991) Design for Environment: A New Strategy for Environmental Management. *Pollution Prevention Review.* Winter, 1991-92.

Altieri, M. A. (1993) Sustainable Rural Development in Latin America: Building from the Bottom Up. *Ecological Economics.* 7; April, pp 93-121.

Amanor Kajo, (1994) *The New Frontier: Farmer Responses to Land Degradation*, Zed Books.

Angell, D.J.R., Comer, J.D. and Wilkinson, M.L.N. (eds.) (1990) *Sustaining Earth: Response to Environmental Threats.* Basingstoke: Macmillan.

Archibugi, F. and Nij Kamp, P. (eds.) (1989) *Economy and Ecology: Towards Sustainable Development.* Dardrect, Netherlands: Kluwer Academic.

Arias, M. (1992) Mothering the Earth. *Development.* 1; pp. 75-78.

Arnold. S. H. (1989) Sustainable Development: A Solution to the Development Puzzle. *Development*, 2 (3); pp. 26.

Ashis, Madhara. (1989) Resource Management by the People for the People. *Journal of Land Management.* 1(3); July-September, p. 76.

Ashraf, Ali. (1993) Gandhian View of Sustainable Development. *Indian Journal of Public Administration.* 39 (3); July-September, p. 265.

Ausubel, J.H. (1992) Industrial Ecology: Reflections on a Colloquium. *Proceedings of National Academy of Sciences*, 89; February.

Axinn, George. (1991) Sustainable Development Reconsidered. *Development.* 1; p. 120.

Baier A. (1980) 'The rights of past and future persons', in Partridge, E. (ed.) *Responsibilities to Future Generations.* Buffalo, New York: Prometheus.

Bairnes, Douglas F. and Jose Olivares. (1988) *Sustainable Resource Management in Agriculture and Rural Development Projects*: A Review of Bank Policies,

Procedures and Results, Environment Department, Working Paper no, 5, Washington DC: World Bank.

Baneca, J.J. (1974) *Environmental Economics.* 2nd ed. Englewood Cliffs, N.J: Prentice-Hall.

Banes, Peter (1992) *Dissent on Development.* Cambridge: Harvard University Press.

Bapna, Amit. (1993) Indian Attitudes to Environment : Past and Present. *Development*, 2; p. 74.

Barbier, E.B. and A. Markandya. (1989) *The Conditions for Achieving Environmentally Sustainable Economic Development.* LEEC Paper 89-01, London: London Environmental Economics Centre.

Barbier, Edward B. (1989). *Economics, Natural Resource Scarcity and Development.* London: Earthscan Publication.

Barbier, E. (1987), The Concept of Sustainable Economic Development, *Environmental Conservation.* 14.

Barbier, E. (1981) *Sustainable Resource Management as a Factor in International Economic Security.* Paper presented at Centre for Economic Policy Research Workshop on Economic Aspects of International Security, London.

Barnes, D.F. (1988) *Sustainable Resources Management in Agriculture and Rural Development Projects: A Review of Bank Policies*, Proceedings, Results. Washington : World Bank Environment Department.

Barnet, H. and C. Morse. (1963), *Scarcity and Growth: The Economics of Natural Resource Availability.* Baltimore: Leo John Hopkins University Press.

Barraclough, S. (1991). *The Social Origins of Poverty and Food Strategies.* London: Zed Books.

Bartelmus, P. (1994) *Environment, Growth and Development: The Concepts and Strategies of Sustainability.* London & New York: Routledge.

Batisse, M. (1982). The Biosphere Reserve: A Tool for Environmental Conservation and Management. *Environmental Conservation.* 9, 101-11

Batubenga, N.K. (1993) Women and the Environment. *Development.* 2; 1993. p. 79.

Baumol, W.J. and W.E. Oates. (1979) *Economics, Environmental Policy and the Quality of Life.* Englewood Cliffs, New Jersey: Prentice Hall.

Baver, Peter T. (1972) *Dissent on Development*, Cambridge MA: Howard View, Press.

Bebbington, Anthony. (1993) Sustainable Livelihood Development in the Andes. *Development Policy Review*. 11(1); March, 1993. p. 5.

Becker, Robert. (1982) Intergenerational Equity, The Capital—Environment Trade-off. *Journal of Environmental Economics and Management*. 9 (2); 1982.

Beckerman, W. (1992) Economic Growth and the Environment: Whose Growth? Whose Environment? *World Development* 20, 481-96.

Beckerman, Wilfred. (1992) 'Economic Development and the Environment: Conflict or Complementarity?, Background Paper, *World Development Report*. 1982, Development and the Environment.

Bhagat, R. K. (1993) Issues of Calcutta's West Lands. *Yojana*. 36 (24); January 15, p. 17.

Bhagat. R. K. (1991) Sunder Bans: *Yojana*. 35 (22); December, 15, pp. 20-23.

Bhatt, M.G. (1991) Property Rights and Forest Preservation. *American Journal of Agricultural Economics*. 73(2); May, p. 375.

Bhattacharya, H.C. (1991) Nutrient Balance and Sustainable Agriculture. *Fertiliser News*. 36 (6), June.

Bhattacharya, K.P. (1992) Sustainable Indian Mega-Cities. *Nagarlok*. 24(4); October-December, p. 31.

Bhowmik, K.L. (ed.) (1988) *Urban Development*. New Delhi: Inter-India Publication.

Bilal, Babar. (1993) Environment Related Legislation on Land Use and Water Quality in Pakistan. *Development*. 2; p. 76.

Bishop, R.C. (1978) Economics of Endangered Species, *American Journal of Agricultural Economics*. 60, 10-18.

Biswas, P. K. (1993) Forestry-based Sustainable Development. *Indian Journal of Public Administration* 39 (3); July-September, p. 473.

Blaikie, P. and Brookfield, H. (1987) *Land Degradation and Society*. London: Methuen.

Boulding, K.E. (1966) 'The Economics of the Coming Spaceship Earth', in *Environmental Quality in a Growing Economy* (reprinted in) H.E. Daly (ed.) (1973) Towards a Steady—

State Economy, New York: W.H. Freeman.

Boulding, Kenneth. (1964) *The Entropy Trap in the Meaning of the Twentieth Century*. New York: Harper and Row.

Bowers, J. (1997) *Sustainability and Environmental Economics: An Alternative Text*. England: Longman.

Brandland, H. (1989) Sustainable Development : An Overview. *Development*. 2 (3); p. 13.

Brandt Commission. (1980) *North-South: A Programme for Survival*. London: Pan.

Brittain, Robert. (1968) *Let there be Bread*. London: Spading & Levy.

Bromley, D.W. (1992) The Commons, Common Property and Environmental Policy, *Environmental and Resource Economics*. 2, 1-18.

Brookfield, H.C. (1991) Environmental Sustainability with Development. *Development*. 1; p. 113.

Brookfield, H. (1991) Environmental Sustainability with Development: What prospects for a research agenda? *European Journal of Development Research*. 3, pp. 41-67

Brown, L. (1981) *Building a Sustainable Society*. New York: Norton.

Brown, L.R. (1993) 'A new era unfolds' in L.R. Brown *et al.*, *State of the World 1993*, A Worldwatch Institute Report on Progress towards a Sustainable Society, New York and London: Norton.

Bullard, Clark W. (1995) The Energy Costs of Goods and Services. *Energy Policy*. 3 (4); 268, December.

Capra, F. S. C. (1993) Green Politics: A New Paradigm. *Phi Kappa Phi Journal*. May 12.

Carley, Michael. (1992) *Managing Sustainable Development*. London : Earthscan.

Carr-Harris, J. (ed.) (1994) *Global View of the Environment: Two Years after Rio*. New Delhi: South-South Solidarity.

Carr-Harris, Jill. (1992) *Agriculture and People: Eco-health Hazards of Chemical Based Agricultural*. New Delhi: South-South Solidarity.

Cavalcanti, C. (1991) *Government Policy and Ecological Concerns: Some Lessons from the Brazilian Experience*. New York: Columbia University Press.

Chakravarty, S. (1992) *Sustainability: The Concept and its*

Economic Application in the Context of India. New Delhi: Centre for Science and Environment.

Chakravarty, Sukhmay. (1992) Sustainability: The Concept and its Economic Application in the context of India, in Agarwal Anil. (eds.) *The Price of Forests*: Proceedings of a seminar on the Economics of the Sustainable use of Forest Resources, New Delhi: Centre for Science and Environment.

Chambers, R.&G. Conway. (1992) Towards an ecological economics and sustainability, *Ecological Economics*. pp. 6, 7-34.

Chambers, R., N.C. Saxena and T. Shah. (1989) *To The Hands of the Poor: Water and Trees*. New Delhi and London: Oxford and IBH.

Chapman, Duane. (1991) Environment, Production, Resource Depletion, and the Sustainability of Developing Country Agriculture. *Economic Development and Cultural Change*. 39(4); July, p. 723.

Chapman, P. F. (1974) Energy Costs: A Review of Methods. *Energy Policy*, June.

Chase, Brian F. (1993) Tropical Forests and Trade Policy. *Third World Quarterly*. 4(4); November, p. 449.

Chaturvedi, R.S. (1989) Remote Sensing in the Management of Natural Resources. *Journal of Land Management* 1 (3); July-September, p. 45.

Chenoy, Kamal. (1993) Sustainable Development in India. *Indian Journal of Public Administration*. 39. (3); July-September, p. 282.

Chitale, M. A. (1991) Environmental Management in Water Resources Projects: Indian Experiences of Irrigation and Power Projects. *Journal of Indian Water Resources Society*. 11(1); January, p. 6.

Chitepo, Victoria. (1991) Population, Women and Environment. *Development*. 1; p. 124.

Ciriacy-Wantrup, S.V. (1963) *Resource Conservation* Berkeley: University of California Press.

Clark, W.C. and Munn, R.E. (eds.) (1986) *Sustainable Development of the Biosphere*. Cambridge: Cambridge University Press.

Clerk, Robin. (1983) *Human-Environment: Action or Disaster*. Dublin: Tycooly.

Cobb, John. (1992) *Ecology, Ethics and Theology*. Cambridge: MIT Press.

Cointreu, S.J.(1982) *Environmental Management of Urban Solid Wastes in Developing Countries: A Project Guide*. Washington: Urban Development Department, The World Bank.

Colcheser, Marcus. (1994) Sustaining the Forests. *Development & Change*. 25(1); January, p. 69.

Colchester, M. and L. Lohmann. (ed.) (1993) *The Struggle for Land and the Fate of the Forest*. Penang, Malaysia : The World Rainforest Movement.

Collard, D. (*et al.*) (eds.) (1988) *Economics, Growth and Sustainable Environments*. London: Macmillan.

Collard, D., D. Pearce and D. Ulph. (1988) *Economics, Growth and Sustainable Environments: Essays in Memory of Richard Lecomber*. New York: St. Martin's Press.

Collicott, J. B. (1992) *Aldo Leopold's Metaphor*. Washington: Island Press.

Conrad, Jon M. (1987) *Natural Resource Economics: Notes and Problems*. New York: Cambridge University.

Conroy, Czech. (1998) Sustainable Development—Making It Happen. *Appropriate Technology*. 16 (2); September, pp. 1-4.

Cook, E. (1980) *Limits to Exploitation of Non-Renewable Resources*. San Francisco: W. H. Freeman & Co.

Costanza, R. and H.E., Daly, (1992) Natural Capital and Sustainable Development, *Conservation Biology*. pp. 6, 37-46.

Costanza, R. (1992) *Toward an Operational Definition of Ecosystem Health*. Washington DC: Island Press.

Cromwell, E. (1991) Modern Varieties and Sustainable Development. *Journal of International Development*. 3 (5) October, p. 551.

Cropper, M.L. (1992) Environmental Economics: A Survey: *Journal of Economics Literature*. 30; June.

D'Arge, R. C. (1991) *Economic Strategies for Mitigating the Impacts of Climate Change on Future Generations*. New York: Columbia University Press.

Dahlbery, K. A. (1986) *Natural Resources and People: Conceptual Issues in Interdisciplinary Research*. London:

West View.

Daly, H. E. (1993) *Sustainable Growth: An Impossibility Theorem*. London: MIT Press.

Daly, H. E. (1990) Sustainable Growth: An Impossibility Theorem. *Development*. 3 (4); p. 45.

Daly, H.E. and J.B. Cobb Jr. (1990) *For the Common Good: Redirecting the Economy towards Community, the Environment and a Sustainable Future*. London: Green Print.

Daly, H. E. (1980) *On Economics as a Life Science*. San Francisco: W.H. Freeman & Co.

Daly, H. E. (1973) *Electric Power, Employment and Economic Growth: A Case Study in Growthmania*. San Francisco: W. H. Freeman & Co.

Dankelman, Irena. (1991) Sustainable Development. *Development*. 1; p. 134.

Dasgupta, Biplab. (1977) *The New Agrarian Technology and India*. Delhi: Macmillan.

Dasmann, Raymond F. (1959) *Environmental Conservation*. 3rd ed. New York: Wiley.

Davis, Ted J. and Isabel Schirmer. (1987) Sustainability Issues in Agricultural Development: Proceedings of the Seventh Agricultural Sector Symposium, Washington DC: World Bank.

de la Court, T. (1990) *Beyond Brundtland: Green Development in the 1990s*. London: Zed Books.

Dhabriya, S.S. (1988) *Desert Spread and Desertification: An Analysis of the Identified Aravalli Gaps on the Desert Fringe*. Jaipur : Environmentalists.

Dhabriya, S.S. (1988) Eco-crisis in the Aravalli hill region: Changing Environmental Status and Proposed Remedial Measures for its Generation. Jaipur : Environmentalists.

Dhawan, B. D. (1993) Sustaining Ground Water-based Agriculture in India. *Journal of Public Administration*. 39 (3); July-September, p. 435.

Dixon, J.A. (1989) *The Concept of Sustainability, Origins, Extension and Usefulness for Policy*. Washington: World Bank Environmental Department.

Dommen, E. (ed.) (1993), *Fair Principles for Sustainable Development*, Published for UNCTAD. Hants: Edward Elgar

Publishing Ltd.

Dorfman, R. (1991) Protecting the Global Environment. *World Development.* 19 (1); January, p. 103.

Dovers, S. (1989) Sustainability: Definitions, Clarifications and Contexts. *Development.* 2 (3); p. 33.

Dusik, Jiri. (1993) Environment Protection in Czechoslovakia. *Development,* 2; p. 83.

Dwivedi, O. P. (1989) *Satyagraha for Conservation: Awakening the Spirit of Hinduism.* London : Belhaven Press.

Earls, Felton. (1993) Towards Sustainable Development for American Families. *Daeddus.* 122 (1); Winter, p. 93.

Eckholm, Eric. (1979) *Planning for the Future: Forestry for Human Needs.* Washington: Worldwatch Institute.

Ekins, Paul. (1991) A Strategy for Global Environmental Development. *Development.* 2; p. 64.

Elkington, John. (1994) Sustainable Development with Special Reference to Environment and Agriculture. *Indian Journal of Rural Development* 13 (1); January-March, p. 47.

Engel, J.R. and J.G. Engel. (eds.) (1989) *Ethics of Environment and Development.* London: Belhaven Press.

Esteva, Gustavo. (1992) Grassroots Resistance to Sustainable Development, *The Ecologist.* 22(2); March-April, p. 45.

FAO, UNFPA, IIASA. (1982) *Population Supporting Capacities of Lands in the Developing World.* FAO, Rome.

Farmer, B. A. (1974) *Agricultural Colonization in India since Independence.* London: Oxford University Press.

Fletcher, W. W. (ed.) (1979) *Economics of the Environment.* London: Blackie.

FRI. (1961) *Hundred Years of Indian Forestry 1861.* Dehradun: Forest Research Institute.

FSI. (1988) *State of India's Forests,* Dehradun: Forest Survey of India.

Gadgil, Madhav. (1993) Restoring India's Forest Wealth. *Indian Journal of Public Administration.* 39 (3); July-September, p. 586.

Gadgil Madhav and Ramachandra Guha, (1992) *This Fissured Land: An Ecological History of India.* Oxford University Press.

Galtung, J. (1984) Perspectives on Environmental Politics in Overdeveloped and Underdeveloped Countries. In B. Glaeser (ed.), *Eco-development: Concepts,* Projects, Strategies. Oxford: Pergamon Press.

Ganeshwar, V. (1992) Sustainable Urban Development. *Nagarlok.* 24(4); October-December, p. 21.

Gaon, Narottam. (1993) Environment & Development. *Indian Journal of Public Administration.* 39 (3); July-September, p. 300.

George, Susan. (1988) *A Fate Worse than Debt.* Harmondsworth: Penguin.

Ghai, D. and J.M. Vivian. (1993) *Grassroots Environmental Action: People's Participation in Sustainable Development.* London: Routledge.

Giddens, A. (1990) *The Consequences of Modernity.* Cambridge: Polity Press.

Global 2000: Report to the President. (1980) Washington DC: U.S. Government Printing Office.

GOI. (1988) India: Environmental Hygiene Committee Report: October, 1988, Simla: Government of India Press.

Goodland R. (*et al.*) (eds.) (1992) *Environmentally Sustainable Economic Development: Building on Bruntland.* Environmental Working Paper no. 46, Washington, DC: World Bank

Goodland, Robert. (*et al.*) (1990) *Tropical Moist Forest Management : The Urgent Transition to Sustainability.* Washington DC: The World Bank.

Gore, A. (1992) *Earth in Balance: Forging a New Common Purpose.* Earthscan: London.

Gorizontoy, Borie. (1985) *Capitalism and the Ecological Crisis.* Moscow: Progress.

Gowariker, Vasant. (1994) Redefining the Good Society. *Economic and Political Weekly.* 29(23); January 2, pp. 1383-85.

Gowda, M.V.S. (1992) What is Sustainable Development. *Employment News.* July 18-24.

Gradwohl Judith. (1988) *Sustainable Agriculture-Tropics.* Earthscan Publications.

Grove, P. (1990) Threatened Islands, Threatened Earth: Early Professional Science and the Historical Origins of Global Environment Concerns. In Angell, D.J.R., Coomer, J.D. and Wilkinson, K.L.N. (eds.), *Sustaining Earth: Response to*

Environmental Threats. Basingstoke: Macmillan.

Guha, Ramachandra (1989) The Unquiet Woods : *Ecological Change and Peasant Resistance in the Himalayas*. Oxford University Press.

Gupta, N. L. and R. K. Gujjar. (eds.) (1993) *Sustainable Development*. Jaipur: Rawat Publications.

Gupta, R.G. (1992) Public-Private Cooperation for Sustainable Urban Development: A Case Study of Delhi. *Nagarlok*. 24(4); October-December, p. 83.

Gurung, Barun. (1992) Towards Sustainable Development. *Futures*. 24 (9) 1 November, p. 90.

Gusain, P. P. S. (1990) *Renewable Energy in India*. New Delhi: Vikas Publishing House.

Gyawali Kipak. (1991) Energizing Development and Sustaining the Environment. *Development*. 1; p. 129.

Hallsworth, B. G. (ed.) (1982) *Socio-Economic Effects and Constraints in Tropical Forest Management*. New York: John Wiley & Sons.

Haque, M.M. (1991) Sustainable Development and Environment. *Project Appraisal*. 6 (3); September, pp. 149-57.

Hardin, G. (1991) Paramount Positions in Ecological Economics, 'in R. Constanza (ed.) *Ecological Economics: The Science and Management of Sustainability*. New York: Columbia.

Hardoy, G.E. (1992) *Environmental Problems in Third World Cities*. London; Earthscan.

Hays, S.P. (1959) *Conservation and the Gospel of Efficiency*. Cambridge MA: Harward University Press.

Helm, D. (ed.) (1991) *Economic Policy towards the Environment*. Oxford: Blackwell.

Henderson, J. V. (1988) *Urban Development: Theory, Fact, and Illusion*. New York: Oxford University Press.

Heyzer Noeleen. (ed.) (1988) *Daughter in Industry*: Work, Skills and Consciousness of Women Workers in Asia, Asian Pacific Development Centre.

Heyzer Noeleen. (ed.) (1987) Women Farmers and Rural Change in Asia, Asian Pacific Development Centre.

Hiemstra, W. (ed.) (1992) *Let Farmers Judge: Experiences in Assessing the Sustainability of Agriculture*. London: Intermediatĕ Technology Pub.

Hildyard, Nicolas. (1991) The Hunger Machine. *The Ecologist*. 21

(6); November-December, pp. 239-43.

Hirsch, Fred. (1977) *Social Limits to Growth*. London: Routledge and Kegan Paul.

Hoberry, J. (1990) Natural Resource Management for Sustainable Development. *Journal of International Development*. 2 (4); October, p. 449.

Holdgate, M. (1991). The Environment of Tomorrow. *Environment* 33, 14-20;

Holmberg, J., Bass, S. and Timberlake, L. (1991) *Defending the Future: A Guide to Sustainable Development*. London: International Institute for Environment and Development.

Hughes, D. (1983) Gaia: an Ancient View of Our Planet. *The Ecologist*. pp. 13, 2-3.

Hussain, Akmal. (1990) Resource Base Erosion and Sustainable Development in South Asia. *Economic and Political Weekly*. 25 (33); August 18, pp. 1847-1815.

Hussain, Akmal (1989) Sustainable Development and Regional Cooperations. *Mainstream*. 27 (39); June, pp. 18-22.

Inamdar, N. R. (1993) Sustainable Development. *Indian Journal of Public Administration*. 39 (3); July-September, p. 372.

Inter-Secretariat Working Group on National Accounts. (1994) *System of National Accounts* 1993 Brussels/Luxembourg, New York, Paris, Washington, DC: United Nations Publications.

ISS. (1994) *Development and Change*, Special Issue: Development and Environment: Sustaining People and Nature, Vol. 25, no.1, Jan. 1994, the Hague: Institute of Social Studies.

IUCN/UNEP/WWF. (1991) *Caring for the Earth: A Strategy for Sustainable Living*. Switzerland: IUCN.

IUCN/UNEP/WWF. (1980) *The World Conservation Strategy, International Union for Conservation of Nature and Natural Resources*. Geneva: United Nations Environment Programme, World Wildlife Fund.

Jacobs, M. (1991) *The Green Economy*. London: Pluto Press.

Jacobson, J.L. (1993) *Closing the Gender Gap in Development*, in L.R. Brown (*et al.*) *State of the World 1993*. A Worldwatch Institute Report on Progress Toward a Sustainable Society. New York & London: Norton.

Jazairy, I. (1987) How to make Africa self sufficient in food.

Journal of the Society of International Development 2 (3), 50-4.

Joekes Susan, (1987) *Women in the World Economy*, Oxford University Press.

John, Adedokum. (1992) The Informal Sector & Sustainable Urban Development in the Nigeria. *Nagarlok.* 24(4); October-December, p. 69.

Jordan, A. (1993) *The Global Environment Facility*, Working Paper, GEC 92-37, Centre for Social and Economic Research on the Global Environment, University of East Anglia, Norwich.

Joshi, P.K. (1991) Sustainability of Existing Farming System in Punjab & Haryana: Some Issues on Ground Water Use. *Indian Journal of Agriculture Economics.* 46(3), July-September, p. 412.

Joshi. G.V. (1992) Sustainable Rural Development for Sustainable Urban Development. *Nagarlok.* 24(4); October-December, p. 69.

Kamta, Prasad. (1993) Sustainable Development of Drought-Prone Areas. *Indian Journal of Public Administration* 39(3); July-September, p. 454.

Kemp, Rene. (1992) The Greening of Technological Progress. *Future.* 24(5) 1 July, pp. 437-57.

Khanna, G. N. (1990) *Environment Problems and the United Nations.* New Delhi: Ashish.

Kirkby, J., O'Keefe, P. and L. Timberlake. (1995) *The Earthscan Reader in Sustainable Development.* London: Earthscan.

Krishnaji, P. (1992) Social Banking and Sustainable Development. *Monthly Commentary.* 33(8); March, pp. 61-65.

Kumar. R. (1987) *Environmental Pollution and Health Hazards in India.* New Delhi : Ashish.

Lal, Padma. (1994) Sustainable Development in the Pacific Islands: *Development Bulletin.* 31st July, p. 50.

Leiss, W. (1986) *The Limits to Satisfaction.* Toronto: University of Toronto Press.

Lovdiyi D., Nagle W., and Ofosu-Amauh. (1989) The African Women's Assembly: *Women and Sustainable Development.* Washington DC: World Wide.

Lubell, Harold. (1982) *Urban Development and Employment: The Prospects for Calcutta.* New Delhi: Concept Publishing.

Luoma, Samuel N. (1984) *Introduction to Environmental Issues.* New York: Macmillan.

Lutz, E. (1992) Integration of Environmental Concerns into Agricultural Policies. *World Development.* 20(2); February, pp. 241-53.

Mahapatra, S. (1993) Ecological Farming: Concept & Techniques. *Kurukshetra.* 41(10); July, p. 26.

Maitra, A.K. (1992) Fuelwood and Energy Sources for Village Communities of Mountain Areas: A Case Study of Kulu District in Agarwal, A. (ed.) *The Price of Forests.* New Delhi: Centre for Science and Environment.

Manrya, S. D. (ed.). (1989) *Urbanisation and Environmental Problems.* Allahabad: Change Publications.

Mardista, P. (1993) Sustainable Development for Estonia: Why Not? *Development.* 2; p. 72.

Marien, Michael. (1992) Environmental Problems and Sustainable Futures. *Futures.* 24(8); October.

Markandaya, Anil. (1992) *Policies for Sustainable Development.* FAO.

Mayur, Rashmi. (1992) NGO Movement for Evaluation to Continue for Millions of Years to Come. *Nagarlok*: 24(4); October-December, p. 106.

Meadows, D. H. (*et al.*), (1972) *The Limits to Growth.* New York: Universe Books.

Menaria, Rajendra. (1989) *Environmental Conservation and Planning.* New Delhi: Ashish.

Mikesell Raymond F. (1992) *Economic Development and the Environment.* New York: Monsell Publishing Ltd.

Mikesell, Raymond F. and Lawrence F. Williams. (1992) *The International Banks and the Environment: From Growth to Sustainable Development—An Unfinished Agenda.* San Franisco: Sierra Club Books.

Miles, I. (1985) *Social Indicators for Human Development.* London: Francis Pinter.

Miller, Moris. (1990) Can Development be Sustainable. *Development.* 2 (4); p. 28.

Mishra, S.N. (1993) People's Participation for Sustainable Development. *Indian Journal of Public Administration* 39 (3); July-September, p. 254.

Misra, Girish K. (1993) Sustainable Urban Development and

Privatisation. *Indian Journal of Public Administration* 39(3); July-September, p. 538.

Misra, R. P. (1993) Sustainable Development—The Ecological Perspectives. *Indian Journal of Public Administration* 39 (3); July-September, p. 254.

Mukherjee, A. and V. K. Agnihotri. (eds). (1993) *Environment and Development: View from the East and the West.* New Delhi: Concept.

Muttagi, P. K. (1991) Sustainable Development. *Quarterly Journal of All India Institute of Local Self-Government.* Bombay. 62 (364); July-December, pp. 122-40.

Nadkarni, M. V. (1993) Sustainable Development. *Indian Journal of Agricultural Economics.* 48 (3); July-Sept., p. 516.

Nag, C.B.D. (1987) *Global Environment Movement: New Hope for Mankind.* New Delhi: Sterling.

Nayak, A.K. (1993) Sustainable Agriculture : Some Observations. *Yojana.* 37(22); December 15, p. 7.

Ninan, K.N. (1993) Green Revolution Dryland Agriculture & Sustainability. *Economic & Political Weekly.* 28 (12&13): March 20-27.

Nordhaus, W. (1992) *Is Growth Sustainable?* Reflection on the concept of sustainable economic growth, Paper Presented to International Economic Association Meeting, Varenna, Italy, October.

Norton, B.G. (1992) Sustainability, Human, Welfare and Ecosystem Health. *Environmental Values.* 1, 97-111.

Odum, E.P. (1971) *Fundamentals of Ecology.* Philadelphia: W.B. Saunders.

OECD. (1991) *The State of the Environment Report,* Paris: Organisation for Economic Cooperation and Development.

Ostrom, E. (1990) *Governing the Commons: The Evolution of Institutions for Collective Action.* Cambridge: Cambridge University Press.

Pal, B. P. (1992) *Environmental Conservation and Development.* Dehradun: Natraj.

Palnitkar, Sneha. (1993) Intermediate City Towards the Sustainable Urban Development. *Journal of the All India Institute of Local Self-government.* 64(2); January-June, pp. 79-83.

Panigrahi A. & K. Mukundon. (1992) Environmental Implications of Urban Development, *Nagarlok*. Vol. XXIV, No. 4, Oct-Dec.

Parikh, K.S. (1993) *Human Development & Natural Resource-Structural Adjustment*. Madras: Macmillan.

Park, C. (ed.) (1986) *Environmental Policies: Introductional Review*. London: Croom Helm.

Patil, Vinayak. (1991) Role of Cooperatives in Preservation of Environment and Ecology for Sustainable Development. *Cooperative Perspective*. 26(2); July-September, p. 206.

Patkar, V.N. (1992) Systems Interdependence as a Determinant of Sustainable Urban Development. *Nagarlok*. Vol. XXIV, No. 4, Oct-Dec.

Pearce, D.W. (ed.) (1995) *Blue Print 4: Sustaining the Earth: Capturing Global Value*, London: Earthscan.

Pearce, D.W. (ed.) (1994) *Blue Print 3: Measuring Sustainable Development*. London: Earthscan.

Pearce, D.W. and Atkinson, G.D.(1992) Are National Economics Sustainable: Measuring Sustainable Development. CSERGE GEC Working Paper 92-11, CSERGE, UEA, London: Norwich and UCL.

Pearce, D.W. (ed.) (1991) *Blueprint 2: Greening the World Economy*. London: Earthscan.

Pearce, David & Warford Jeremy (1991) *Environment and Economic Development*. Oxford University Press for the World Bank.

Pearce David, Edward Barbier & Anil Markandya. (1990) *Sustainable Development, Economics and Environment in the Third World*. London Environmental Economics Centre, England: Edward Elgar Publishing Ltd.

Pearce, D.W. and R.K. Turner, (1990) *Economics of Natural Resources and the Environment*. Harvester Wheatsheaf, Henrel, Hempstead.

Pearce, David. (1990) *Sustainable Development: Economics & Environment in the Third World*. Hants: Edward Edgar.

Pearce, David, Anil Markandya and Edward B. Barbier, (1989) *Blue Print for a Green Economy*. London: Earthscan Publications.

Pezzey, J. (1989) *Definitions of Sustainability*, Working Paper no. 9 London: UK Centre for Environment and Development.

Pezzey, J. (1989) *Economic Analysts of Sustainable Growth and*

Sustainable Development. Environment Department, Working Paper No. 15 Washington, DC: World Bank,

Pezzey, J. (1992) Sustainability: An Interdisciplinary Guide, *Environmental Values.* pp. 1, 321-61.

Pirage, D. C. (1977) *Sustainable Society, Implications for Limited Growth.* New York: Praeger.

Potter, Robert B. (1985) *Urbanisation and Planning in the Third World: Spatial Perceptions and Public Participation.* London: Croom House.

Prakash, Daman. (1991) The Role of Cooperatives in Preservation of Environment & Ecology for Sustainable Development. *Cooperative Perspective.* 26(2); July-September, p. 210.

Prasad, Kamta. (1993) Sustainable Development of Drought-Prone Area. *Indian Journal of Public Administration* 39 (3); July-September, p. 454.

Raj, Mulkh. (1992) Sustainable Urban Development. *Nagarlok.* 24(4); October-December, p. 1.

Raj, P. J. Sanjeeva. (1993) Sustainable Development of the Pulicat Lake India. *Social Action.* 43(2); April-June, p. 225.

Rajasekaran, B. (1991) Indigenous Natural-Resource Management Systems for Sustainable Agricultural Development. *Journal of International Development.* 3(4); July, p. 387.

Raju, B. Yerram. (1993) Project Sustainability. *Prashasnika.* 20(1-2); January-December, p. 95.

Ram Nandan and P. Sinha. (eds.) (1990) *Environment and Human Response: Selected Essays in Geography,* New Delhi: Concept.

Ramachandran, Arcot. (1992) Transportation and Sustainable Development. *Nagarlok.* 24(40); October-December. p. 149.

Ramachandran, H. (1990) (ed.) *Environmental Issues in Agricultural Development.* New Delhi : Concept Publishing Company.

Ramachandran, Nira. (1996) How Sustainable is Out Food Security in V.K. Agnihotri and H. Ramachandran (ed.) *Dimensions of the New Economic Policy,* Vol. 2, New Delhi: Concept Publishing Company.

Ramchand, K. (1992) Environmental Implications of Urban Development. *Nagarlok.* 24(4); October-December, p. 51.

Randhawa, M. S. (1964) *Farmers of India.* New Delhi: ICAR.

Redclift, M. (1987) *Sustainable Development: Exploring the Contradictions.* London: Methuen.

Reganold, John P. (1990) Sustainable Agriculture. *Scientific American*. 262(6); June, pp. 112-121.

Reid, D. (1995) *Sustainable Development: An Introductory Guide*. London: Earthscan.

Repetto, Robert. (1992) Key Elements of Sustainable Development, Background Paper, *World Development Report*. Development and Environment, New York: Oxford University Press.

Repetto, R. Magrath W., Wells, M., Beer, C. and Rossini, F. (1989) *Wasting Assets, National Resources in the National Income Accounts*. Washington DC: World Resources Institute.

Repetto, Robert (*et al.*) (1989) *Wasting Assets: Natural Resources in the National Income Accounts*. Washington, DC: World Resources Institute.

Repetto, R and Gillis, M. (eds.) (1988) *Public Policies and the Misuse of Forest Resources*, Cambridge UK: Cambridge University Press.

Repetto, R. (1986) *Global Possible: Resources, Development and the New Century*. New Delhi: Segment Book Distribution.

Repetto, R. (1986) *World Enough and Time*, New Haven, Conn: York University Press.

Riddell, R. (1981) *Ecodevelopment*, Aldershot: Gower Publishing.

Roy, Prodipto. (1993) The Death and Life of Sustainable Agro-Forestry. *Indian International Centre Quarterly*. 20(4); Winter, p. 39.

Royston, Michael. (1991) Responsibility of Industry Towards the Environment. *Productivity*. 31(4); January-March, p. 514.

Sachs, I. (1979) Ecodevelopment: A Definition, *Ambio* 8 (2/3), 113.

Sairam, T. V. (1993) Towards Sustainable Development-Regulatory and Fiscal Strategies. *Indian Journal of Public Administration* 39 (3); July-September, p. 406.

Saleth, M. (1994) Sustainable Livelihood Security Index in M.S. Swaminathan (ed.) *Eco-technology and Rural Employment – A Dialogue*. Madras: Macmillan.

Salim, Emil. (1991) Towards a Sustainable Future. *Development* 2; p. 61.

Sapru, R. K. (1988) *Environment Planning and Management in*

India. New Delhi: Commonwealth.

Saxena. N.C. (1993) Sustainable Development of Forest Lands and Joint Forest Management in India. *Indian Journal of Public Administration* 39(3); July-September, p. 465.

Schafer, D. and Stahmer, C. (1990) Conceptual Considerations on Satellite Systems, *Review of Income and Wealth*, 36, 2: 167-76.

Schurter, Dale. (1971) *World Crisis in Agriculture*. California: Ambassador College Press.

Sedjo , R.A. (1992) A Global Forestry Initiative. *Resources*. 109, 16-18.

Shah, S.M. (1992) Towards Sustainable Development. *Yojana*, 36(16); September, 15, pp. 18-21.

Shah, Tushaar. (1993) Institutional Foundations of Natural Resources Management. *Indian Journal of Public Administration*. 39(3); July-September, p. 603.

Shiva, V. (1991) *The Violence of the Green Revolution: Ecological Degradation and Political Conflict*. London: Zed Books.

Shiva, V. (1989) *Staying Alive:* Women, Ecology and Development. London: Zed Books.

Shrivastava, M. M. P. (1994) Sustainable Development with Special Reference to Environment & Agriculture. *Journal of Rural Development*. 13(1); January-March, p. 47.

Simey, T. S. (1968) *Social Science and Social Purpose*. London: Constable.

Simon, Julian L. & Herman Kahn (eds.) (1984) *The Resourceful Earth*. New York: Basil Blackwell.

Simonis, V.E. (1992) Poverty, Environment and Development. *Monthly Public Opinion Surveys*. 37 (10); July, pp. 1-12.

Singh, Manohar. (1967) *Working Plan for the Tarai and Bhabar Forest Division Western Circle*. Uttar Pradesh, 1965-66 to 1974-75. Nainital: Working Plans Circle.

Singh, T.V. (1993) How Sustainable is Sustainable Tourism. *Tourism Recreation Research*. 18(1); p. 1.

Sinha, S.P. (1986) *Urban Environment and Contemporary Ecology*. Ambala Cantt: The Indian Publication.

Sinha, Subir, (1993) Common Property, Collective Action and Ecology. *Economic and Political Weekly*. 28 (27 & 28); July 3-10, pp. 1424-32.

Skreta, Marek. (1992) Environment and Self-sustaining Development. *Monthly Public Opinion Surveys.* 37(10), July, pp. 1-12.

Sousa, A.D. (ed.) (1978) *The Indian City, Poverty, Ecology and Urban Development.* New Delhi: Manohar Publication.

Spark, R.K. (ed.) (1987) *Environment Management in India*, New Delhi: Ashish.

Stewart, F. (1985) *Planning to Meet Basic Needs.* London: Macmillan.

Stockholm Group for Studies on Natural Resource Management (1988), *Perspectives of Sustainable Development.* Stockholm: Stockholm Group.

Stotter, A.C. (1993) Commodity or Community? Sustainable Development Mountain Resorts. *Tourism Recreation Research.* 18(1); p. 3.

Svendsen Mark and Ruth Meinzen-Dick. (eds.) (1991) *Sources of Future Growth in Indian Irrigated Agriculture. Future Directions for Indian Agriculture.* Research and Policy Issues, Washington DC: International Food Policy Research Institute.

Swaminathan, M.S. (1991) Sustainable Management of Water Resources: Implication for Fact and Livelihood Security. *Journal of Water Resources Society.* 11 (3); July, pp. 1-7.

Theys, J. (1989) *Environmental Accounting in Development Policy: The French Experience*, in Y.J. Ahmed, El Serafy and E. Lutz (eds.) *Environmental Accounting for Sustainable Development.* Washington, DC: the World Bank.

Tietenberg, Thomas H. (1994) *Economics and Environmental Policy.* Aldershot : Edward Edgar.

Tisdell, C. (1988) "Sustainable Development: Different Perspectives of Ecologists and Economists, and Relevance" *World Development.* 16: (3) pp. 373-384.

Toman, M. A. (1992) The Difficulty of Defining Sustainability. *Resources.* 106, 3-6.

Trivedi, S. (1975) *Green Horizons.* New Delhi: Kissan Features Publication.

Turner, R.K. (ed.) (1993) *Sustainable Environmental Economics and Management: Principles and Practice.* London: Belhaven Press.

Turner, R.K. (1992) *Speculations on Weak and Strong*

Sustainability, CSERGE Working Paper, GEC 92-26, University of East Anglia, London: Norwich and University College.

UNESCAP. (1985) Environmental Impact Assessment: Guidelines for Planners and Decision-Makers, Bangkok: UNESCAP.

UNESCO. (1963) *Education and Agricultural Development.* Paris :UNESCO.

UNICEF. (1989) *Children & Environment: UNICEF Strategy for Sustainable Development.* New York: UNICEF.

United Nations. (1993a) *Report of the United Nations Conference on Environment and Development*, Rio de Janeiro, 3-14 June 1992 Vol. 1, New York: United Nations.

United Nations. (1993b) *Integrated Environmental and Economic Accounting*, New York: United Nations.

United Nations. (1983) *Environmental Assessment of Development Projects.* Kuala Lumpur: United Nations. Asian and Pacific Development Centre.

Venkateswarlu, J. (1993) Sustainable Development in Agriculture in West Rajasthan. *Irrigation & Power.* 50 (4); December, p. 121.

W.E. Rees. (1990) *Sustainable Development and Biosphere, Concepts and Principles.* Teilhard Studies No. 23, USA: The American Teilhard Association for the Future of Man, Inc.

Ward, B. and R. Dubos. (1972) *Only One Earth: The Care and Maintenance of a Small Planet.* London: Andre Devrsch.

WCED. (1987) World Commission on Environment and Development, *Our Common Future.* Oxford: Oxford University Press.

Western, D. and M.C. Pearl. (ed.) (1989) *Conservation: Twenty First Century*, New York: Oxford University Press.

Wheeler. J. C. (1991) Development in the Twenty-First Century. *Development.* 1; p. 19.

Williams N.M. and G.B.K. Baines, (eds.) (1993) *Traditional Ecological Knowledge: Wisdom for Sustainable Development.* CRES, Australian National University.

Winpenny, James. (1991) Environmental Values and their Implications for Development. *Development Policy Review.* 9(4); December, pp. 381-90.

World Bank. (1990) "Environmental Policy and Public Revenue in

Developing Countries" *Environment Working Paper 36*. Sector Policy and Research Staff, Environment Department, Washington, DC: World Bank.

World Bank. (1989) *Sub-Saharan Africa from Crisis to Sustainable Growth: A Long-term Perspective Study*. Washington, DC: World Bank.

World Bank. (1985) *Desertification in the Sahelian and Sudanian Zones of West Africa*, Washington, DC: The World Bank.

Wright, David. (1991) Eco-Environmental Policy. *Futures*. 23 (7); September.

Xu, Cheng. (1992) Sustainable Agricultural Development in China. *World Development*. 20(8); August, pp. 1127-44.

INDEX